AMERICAN Pattern Glass TABLE SETS

Identification & Value Guide

Gene and Cathy Florence

Coordinated by
Danny Cornelius **&** Don Jones

COLLECTOR BOOKS
A Division of Schroeder Publishing Co., Inc.

Front cover: Colorado creamer, U.S. Glass Company, c. 1899, emerald w/gold trim, 5⅛" high, 5⅞" across, $95.00. Bird and Strawberry butter dish, Indiana Glass Company, c. 1914, crystal w/bluebirds decoration, 5⅝" high, 7⅜" across, $350.00. Seedpod (Olympia) blue table set, Riverside Glass Works, Wellsburg, West Virginia, 1898: Butter dish, cobalt w/gold trim, 5⅛" high, 7⅝" across, $155.00. Sugar with lid, cobalt w/gold trim, 6⅞" high, 3¾" across, $120.00. Creamer, cobalt w/gold trim, 5⅞" high, 4⅞" across, $85.00. Spooner, cobalt w/gold trim, 4¾" high, 3½" across, $65.00. Westward Ho, Gillinder & Sons, c. 1879: Butter dish, crystal w/frost, 8⅞" high, 7¼" across, $425.00. Sugar with lid, crystal w/frost, 4½" across, $350.00. Creamer, crystal w/frost, 6¾" high, 6" across, $250.00.

Back cover: Cosmos, Consolidated Lamp and Glass Company, c. 1898 – 1905, opaque w/decoration. Butter dish, 5½" high, 8¼" across, $225.00. Sugar with lid, 5¾" high, 4" across, $200.00. Creamer, 4⅝" high, 4¹¹⁄₁₆" across, $175.00. Spooner, 4" high, 3⅜" across, $160.00.

Cover design by Beth Summers
Book design by Heather Warren
Photography by Charles R. Lynch
Glass contributed by Danny Cornelius and Don Jones

COLLECTOR BOOKS
P.O. Box 3009
Paducah, Kentucky 42002-3009

www.collectorbooks.com

Copyright © 2007 Gene and Cathy Florence

The current values in this book should be used only as a guide. They are not intended to set prices, which vary from one section of the country to another. Auction prices as well as dealer prices vary greatly and are affected by condition as well as demand. Neither the authors nor the publisher assumes responsibility for any losses that might be incurred as a result of consulting this guide.

Searching for a Publisher?

We are always looking for people knowledgeable within their fields. If you feel that there is a real need for a book on your collectible subject and have a large comprehensive collection, contact Collector Books.

Proudly printed and bound in the
United States of America

Acknowledgments

A collaborative effort! In a way, every book we've ever worked on has been a collaborative effort, from photographer to proofreaders to printer to shippers; but this one, more so than in the past! This one involved someone else's massive collection (Danny Cornelius and Don Jones), knowledge, enthusiasm, and years of effort obtaining and pouring over materials to learn the intricacies of the subject matter which made the dream of bringing this book to print come true; and although approached by a frustrated Danny at a show with the idea of a source guide depicting actual glass photos which had been born from his own experience of trying to identify patterns using multiple resources, we have had to deal with the feelings of coming to the endeavor less worthy than they because of our skimpier knowledge of this particular field that so fires their zeal! However, after face to face planning discussions and calls and working together at a hectic, concentrated, and involved photo shoot, we have come to understand that, yes, we have played an integral role in the culmination of what began as a hopeful idea! Yes, we inadvertently had some glass to contribute, some catalog information, some insights, and years of photography shoots behind us that helped smooth the way. Also included was some genuine appreciation of this hundred-year-old glass gleaned from past research on items included in our *Pattern Identification* books. Perhaps those four books had engendered the appreciation that allowed us to dare venture beyond our usual focus, which had been concentrated on later glassware from the Depression Era. At any rate, it took all of us, and then some, to put this book before you!

Directly involved was the photographer, Charles R. Lynch, who was key as he spent days trying to obtain the most lucid depictions of each pattern, sometimes scrapping a shot to simply "start over" to show a leg, handle, finial, or faint pattern in a close-up to help fulfill a desire to show the actual pattern. Many previous pattern glass books are filled with black and white artists' depictions which lose so much in translation to the loveliness of the glass itself. Then there were the typists, Amy Sullivan and Beth Ray, who set aside editorial jobs they were involved with to garner information first-hand and to keep up with the sheer magnitude of information being bandied about per item that needed to be included. The book cover artist, Beth Summers, came so she could understand what needed to be addressed as possible candidates for a cover shot, from things easily found to those seldom seen; editor, Gail Ashburn solved problems that could have arisen before they did and saw to our general comfort before we knew it was needed. There was a lithographer, Donna Ballard, working to show us finished shots, lunch "gofers" (previously mentioned) fueling us from flagging under the constant pressure, publisher, Billy Schroeder, interrupting his Memorial Day holiday to help Danny and Don unload their vast collection, carting boxes that had hours of precise cataloguing involved, standing, wrapping, and unwrapping for days in methodical precision. There were phone conversations with knowledgeable people, fellow dealers and friends, Pat Spencer, Evelyn Knowles, Phyllis Petcoff, Mike and Jayne Stoll, and Bettye James, who supplied color and pricing input; and even beyond that were the people who sold sets slated for a book that they may not have been inclined to part with otherwise.

In a note of irony, as collectors, we should note and be encouraged by the fact that although Danny and Don both grew up within a hundred miles of the great glass manufacturing cities of Pittsburgh, Pennsylvania; Wheeling and New Martinsville, West Virginia; Cambridge and Canton, Ohio; it wasn't until moving to Florida that they became interested in early American pattern glass and started what is now their impressive collection.

There was a long line of authors and their written texts preceding us who directly impacted appreciation for the pattern glass table sets we were privileged to be viewing before the camera. In short, this was a collaborative effort from many sources, all with the goal of bringing something worthwhile, something of value to you, the reader; a drive to somehow contribute to the body of knowledge, to share this collection itself and the wonder of being able to collect, appreciate, and preserve glassware that is a tangible art (from the mold makers to the glass craftsmen) from past hands and minds, that has survived from mother's, aunt's, and great grandmother's care for a century. This glass sits with pride among us. Treasure it. Appreciate it; and if need be, rescue it from the shelves of anonymity!

Preface

As with any book, there are issues to address here. The presentation of the glassware herein is a bit unusual in this day and time. We're accustomed to viewing entire settings of glassware. However, in the time frame that this glass represents, it was a common occurrence to have a table set offered, sometimes that being all that was available in that particular design. A "table set" generally consisted of a butter dish and lid, a sugar bowl with lid, a creamer, and a piece called a spooner or spoon holder, which was just that, a dish to hold spoons. It was generally less wide (less than four inches in diameter) than the sugar bowl, had no lid, but might exhibit a top rim with a decorative design (scalloped rim). (There are collectors who concentrate their efforts on spooners alone.) There were also "extended table sets" available which included such extra items as a celery vase or tray, a cruet, or a jelly compote. Having a celery vase at table was considered somewhat of a status symbol back then. Not just everyone had those. They were associated with the more affluent segment of society. Although table sets were originally sold as a set, collectors should know that is often not the way they are found today. Many of the pieces shown in this book were assembled over time, piece by painstaking piece!

Some companies further offered berry and beverage sets to match table sets (note the Indiana Glass catalog pages shown); but some ran the entire gamut of piece selection. Sometimes with berry sets, a second sugar and creamer were offered. These sugar bowls were generally smaller and came without a lid and are referred to as "berry sugars" today. Table sugars came with lids, however, and are priced accordingly. In this book, we have measured creamer heights to the edge of the spout and diameters through the handle width. Since these spouts were molded with the piece and not hand formed, that measurement should be fairly uniform, though we weren't using a caliper, rather a tape measure, to do so. Thus, absolute preciseness may vary.

Notice this photo where we were at pains to turn the lid of a butter dish upside down. This is to show that butter lids often have the pattern inverted from regular items. Thus, you can turn it upright and get the usual image seen, which may assist your identification. Pay attention as you return it to the butter base, however, so that you don't rattle it and produce flakes and chip damage.

Harvard Yard, see p. 86

Where known, we have first listed the factory name or number that applied to that pattern. Otherwise, a name in general use has been incorporated. It's known that some past authors "named" wares and those are the "names" available to us these many years later. Some match the patterns. Others you wonder how in the world they arrived at the name! When patterns from various companies have the same name, we have placed the company producing the pattern before the pattern name. You will also find the abbreviations of OMN and AKA mentioned in this book. The abbreviation OMN stands for "original manufacturer name," and AKA stands for "also known as." In many cases, patterns today are better known by AKA's rather than their original names.

Glassware from this time frame can be found in flint and non-flint varieties. Flint is generally of clearer quality and has more clarity of ring tone. (Don't be thumping some unsuspecting dealer's glassware to establish tonal quality, however, as that is severely frowned upon!) Wait until you own it to establish that. In fact, one of the unnerving-to-the-potential-buyer stories told at the studio was of a seller running around banging a wooden spoon on her glass to "show tone" as part of her sales pitch. Pattern glass shown usually came from a three-piece mold, lines of which can be discovered in the glass itself; and it will most likely glow under a black light from the ore which constituted its original makeup. However, some reproduction artists have carefully incorporated this latter aspect into their wares as well; so this isn't a hundred percent guarantee of age as some would have you believe. All items shown do exhibit this latter property.

Yes, there are later reissues and reproductions to contend with in this field and entire books have been written to address those matters of what exactly to look for in order to ascertain the differences. Where known, we have noted reproductions in the patterns in which they occur. Most of these are well documented elsewhere; refer to the bibliography or your library. Some companies reissued their own wares over years of production; other companies bought original molds or had molds remade of wares and issued them in same and other colors never made originally. Some patterns only have one or two items to contend with; others, rather long listings. However, many of the later issues have concentrated on colors, rather than crystal, in which patterns were often originally manufactured.

Also, because of the ore used in the making of crystal glassware at that time, some pieces will turn lavender or a purple color if placed in direct sunlight over time. The Early American Pattern Glass Society has deemed this devalues the ware significantly. So it would be unwise to court that present trend.

As for condition of the ware, "mint" (original condition from the factory) is preferable and more valuable. Trims (gold, colored flashings, or enamels) should be non-faded, non-scratched, and intact to command the mint prices listed. However, having said that, pieces less than perfect are still worth something to those filling in a set or a collection, just worth less than mint price. After all, the wares are over or near the century mark now — and what shape are *you* going to be in at that point? However, when cracked, glued, or missing finials, handles, feet, spouts, chunks of glass and such, the piece is hardly marketable. Enjoy it on a shelf with a floral arrangement as an item from your family history.

Pricing

Pricing is subject to many variables, such as condition of the glass itself, economic conditions of our time (i.e. cost of gas to seek out shows and finds), prejudices and personal experience of the authors dealing with the glass, popularity of the pattern, and/or number of collectors interested. Prices listed are meant to be a guide only. Glass is more available in some areas than in others and thus will bring more or less in different areas of the country.

The Internet is an everyday tool in today's world. Pricing on the Internet can vary from cheap to astronomical, depending on who is viewing an auction at that moment, who most wants the item or most wants someone else bidding not to have it. However, it is a tool to be considered when locating a particular item and has speeded up the finishing of many collections. It may not always be that way; but right now, possibilities still exist that something you despaired of ever finding may turn up there! If the person has never dealt with glass, you might have to give packing instructions, or it may turn up on your doorstep packed in one sheet of paper and in many pieces, as we have ourselves experienced. (With glass items, we recommend double boxing and triple wrap, one layer of which being bubble wrap. Remember, shipping companies use automated systems which often drop boxes from one conveyor to another from some height in the process of loading and unloading.) Due to having been exported long ago, some of these patterns are found in countries other than ours. When that occurs, remember that shipping fees have to be allowed for in your bidding process. There is definitely still time to obtain "this old glass" all these years later. Even one piece which blesses your eyes every time you see it is worth owning for that reason alone. Collecting is enjoyable. Try it, you'll like it!

Pattern: Actress, OMN: Opera. AKA: Annie, Jenny Lind, Pinafore, Theatrical

Manufacturer: Adams & Company, Pittsburgh, Pennsylvania

Date Introduced: c. 1880

Colors Made: Crystal, crystal w/frost

Reproductions: 9⅛" relish dish often embossed with "IG" logo

Items/Values: Butter dish, crystal, 7¼" high, 6¼" across, $175.00. Creamer, crystal w/frost, 5⅝" high, 5½" across, $95.00.

Not Shown: Sugar with lid, $160.00. Spooner, $75.00.

Pattern: Ada, OMN: Ohio Flint No. 808

Manufacturer: Ohio Flint Glass Company, c. 1897; Cambridge Glass Company, c. 1903

Date Introduced: c. 1897

Colors Made: Crystal

Items/Values: Butter dish, 5¾" high, 8" across, $95.00. Creamer, 4⅝" high, 5⅛" across, $50.00.

Not Shown: Sugar with lid, $50.00. Spooner, $35.00.

Pattern: Adams' Thousand Eye, OMN: Adams' No. 130. AKA: Banded Thousand Eye, Three Knob

Manufacturer: Adams & Company, c. 1874; U.S. Glass Company, c. 1891

Date Introduced: c. 1874

Colors Made: Amber, blue, crystal, vaseline

Items/Values: Butter dish, 6⅝" high, 7⅞" across, $95.00.

Not Shown: Sugar with lid, $75.00. Creamer, pressed, $55.00. Spooner, $45.00.

Notes: Values for plain crystal pieces are 10% less than others. Values given are for amber pieces.

Pattern: Adonis, AKA: Pleat and Tuck, Washboard
Manufacturer: McKee & Brothers, Pittsburgh, Pennsylvania
Date Introduced: c. 1897
Colors Made: Blue, canary, crystal
Items/Values: Butter dish, crystal, 5¼" high, 7⅜" across, $75.00. Sugar with lid, crystal, 7⅜" high, 4½" across, $70.00. Creamer, crystal, 4¾" high, 5⅛" across, $65.00. Spooner, crystal, 4½" high, 3⅜" across, $60.00. Celery vase, crystal, 6½" high, 3⅞" across, $70.00. Milk pitcher, crystal, 7⅜" high, 7" across, $45.00.

Pattern: Aegis, OMN: Swiss. AKA: Bead & Bar Medallion
Manufacturer: McKee & Brothers, Pittsburgh, Pennsylvania; shards found at site of Burlington Glass Works, Hamilton, Ontario, Canada
Date Introduced: c. late 1800s
Colors Made: Crystal
Items/Values: Butter dish, 5⅞" high, 5⅞" across, $95.00. Sugar with lid (no lid shown), 4½" across, $85.00. Creamer, 4⅝" high, 5¼" across, $60.00. Spooner, 4⅜" high, 3⅝" across, $50.00.

Pattern: Aida
Manufacturer: Belmont Glass Company, Bellaire, Ohio (1866 – 1890), listed as Belmont Glass Works in 1888
Date Introduced: c. 1883
Colors Made: Crystal, crystal w/etch
Items/Values: Butter dish, with knife rest, crystal w/etch, 6½" high, 8" across, $175.00. Sugar with lid, crystal w/etch, 8" high, 4¾" across, $125.00. Creamer, crystal w/etch, 6⅛" high, 5½" across, $110.00. Spooner, crystal w/etch, 5⅜" high, 3½" across, $90.00.

Pattern: Alabama, OMN: U.S. Glass No. 15062 – Alabama. AKA: Beaded Bull's Eye and Drape
Manufacturer: U.S. Glass Company, Pittsburgh, Pennsylvania
Date Introduced: c. 1899
Colors Made: Crystal, crystal w/ruby stain
Items/Values: Butter dish, 6⅛" high, 7¾" across, $150.00. Sugar with lid, crystal, 7⅛" high, 4¼" across, $125.00. Creamer, crystal, 4⅞" high, 5½" across, $80.00. Spooner, crystal, 4½" high, 3½" across, $95.00.

Pattern: Alaska, AKA: Lion's Leg
Manufacturer: Northwood Glass Company
Date Introduced: c. 1897
Colors Made: Crystal, emerald, opalescent
Items/Values: Creamer, 3⅜" high, 6¼" across, $125.00.
Not Shown: Butter dish, $400.00. Sugar with lid, $275.00. Spooner, $95.00.
Notes: Values given are for opalescent pieces. Deduct 30% for plain crystal pieces, 10% for emerald pieces.

Pattern: Albion
Manufacturer: Bryce Brothers, c. 1885; U.S. Glass Company, Pittsburgh, Pennsylvania, c. 1891
Date Introduced: c. 1885
Colors Made: Crystal
Items/Values: Butter dish, footed, 5" high, 6½" across, $95.00.
Notes: An example of U.S. Glass Company's special butter dishes, no known matching pieces.

Pattern: Albion
Manufacturer: Bryce Brothers, c. 1885; U.S. Glass Company, Pittsburgh, Pennsylvania, c. 1891
Date Introduced: c. 1885
Colors Made: Crystal
Items/Values: Butter dish, flat, 3¾" high, 7" across, $75.00.
Notes: An example of U.S. Glass Company's special butter dishes, no known matching pieces.

Pattern: Alexis, OMN: Fostoria No. 1630
Manufacturer: Fostoria Glass Company
Date Introduced: c. 1891
Colors Made: Crystal
Items/Values: Sugar with lid, 3¾" across, $50.00. Creamer, 4½" high, 5⅝" across, $40.00. Spooner, 4⅛" high, 3" across, $35.00.
Not Shown: Butter dish, $65.00.

Pattern: Alexis, OMN: Fostoria No. 1630
Manufacturer: Fostoria Glass Company
Date Introduced: c. 1891
Colors Made: Crystal
Items/Values: Cruet w/stopper, 6¾" high with stopper, $70.00.

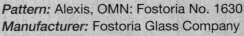

Pattern: Amazon, AKA: Sawtooth, Sawtooth Band
Manufacturer: Bryce Brothers, Pittsburgh, Pennsylvania, 1890 – 1891;
    U.S. Glass Company, Pittsburgh, Pennsylvania at factory "B," c. 1891 – 1904
Date Introduced: c. 1890 – 1891
Colors Made: Crystal, crystal w/etch
Items/Values: Butter dish, crystal, 6" high, 7" across, $80.00. Creamer, crystal, 6⅞"
    high, 4⅝" across, $55.00. Spooner, crystal, 6⅛" high, 3" across, $45.00. Celery
    vase, footed, crystal, 8⅛" high, 3½" across, $55.00.
Not Shown: Sugar with lid, $75.00. Celery vase, flat, $40.00.

Pattern: Anthemion, AKA: Albany
Manufacturer: Model Flint Glass
    Company, Findlay, Ohio
Date Introduced: c. 1895
Colors Made: Crystal,
    crystal/stippled
Items/Values: Sugar with lid,
    crystal, 6½" high, 4" across,
    $60.00. Creamer, crystal, 4⅞"
    high, 5¼" across, $55.00.
    Spooner, crystal, 4½" high, 3¼"
    across, $45.00.
Not Shown: Butter dish, $70.00.

Pattern: Apollo, AKA: Canadian Horseshoe, Frosted Festal Ball, Shield Band, Thumbprint and Prisms
Manufacturer: Adams & Company, Pittsburgh, Pennsylvania, c. 1875; U.S. Glass Company, Pittsburgh, Pennsylvania, at factory "A," c. 1891 – 1899
Date Introduced: c. 1875
Colors Made: Crystal, crystal w/frost finish (plain, etched), crystal w/ruby stain, crystal w/blue, pale yellow, dark green, or any other color is considered rare
Items/Values: Butter dish, crystal w/frost, 6¼" high, 7¼" across, flanged rim, $125.00.
Not Shown: Butter dish, crystal w/frost, plain rim, $70.00. Sugar with lid, $90.00. Creamer, $60.00. Spooner, $45.00.

Pattern: Apollo, AKA: Canadian Horseshoe, Frosted Festal Ball, Shield Band, Thumbprint and Prisms
Manufacturer: Adams & Company, Pittsburgh, Pennsylvania, c. 1875; U.S. Glass Company, Pittsburgh, Pennsylvania, at factory "A," c. 1891 – 1899
Date Introduced: c. 1875
Colors Made: Crystal, crystal w/frost finish (plain, etched), crystal with ruby stain, crystal with blue, pale yellow, dark green, or any other color is considered rare
Items/Values: Butter dish, crystal, 6¼" high, 7½" across, $90.00.
Not Shown: Butter dish, crystal, plain rim, $60.00. Sugar with lid, $55.00. Creamer, $40.00. Spooner, $40.00.

Pattern: Arched Fleur-de-Lis
Manufacturer: Bryce, Higbee & Company, 1898 – 1905; J. B. Higbee Glass Company, 1907
Date Introduced: c. 1898 – 1907
Colors Made: Crystal, crystal w/ruby stain (plain or w/gold)
Items/Values: Butter dish, 5" high, 7¾" across, $85.00. Creamer, crystal, 4⅛" high, 4⅞" across, $55.00. Spooner, crystal, 3⅞" high, 6" across, $55.00. Celery vase, two-handled, crystal, 5⅞" high, 6¾" across handle to handle, $75.00.
Not Shown: Sugar with lid, crystal, $85.00.

Pattern: Arched Ovals, OMN: U.S. Glass Company No. 15091. AKA: Optic, Concave Almond

Manufacturer: U.S. Glass Company, Factory "F" (Ripley & Company), Pittsburgh, Pennsylvania

Date Introduced: c. 1905

Colors Made: Crystal, crystal w/gold, crystal w/ruby stain

Items/Values: Butter dish, 6½" high, 7¾" across, $80.00. Sugar with lid, 7" high, 4¼" across, $75.00. Creamer, 4¾" high, 3¾" across, $60.00. Spooner, 4¼" high, 3½" across, $50.00.

Notes: Values for plain crystal are 10% less than other pieces. Values given are for crystal w/gold pieces.

Pattern: Art, OMN, AKA: Jacob's Tears, Job's Tears, Teardrop and Diamond Block

Manufacturer: Adams & Company, Pittsburgh, Pennsylvania; U.S. Glass Company at factory "A," 1891

Date Introduced: c. 1889

Colors Made: Crystal, crystal w/ruby stain

Reproductions: Compote

Items/Values: Butter dish, crystal, 5⅝" high, 7⅛" across, $90.00. Sugar with lid, crystal, 7¼" high, 4⅛" across, $80.00. Celery vase, crystal, 6½" high, 4" across, $50.00.

Not Shown: Creamer, $75.00. Spooner, $45.00.

Pattern: Ashman, AKA: Cross Roads

Manufacturer: Unknown

Date Introduced: c. 1880s

Colors Made: Crystal, crystal w/etch

Items/Values: Butter dish, crystal, 6¾" high, 5¼" across, $125.00. Sugar with lid, crystal w/etch, 8⅜" high, 3⅞" across, $100.00. Creamer, crystal w/etch, 6¼" high, 6⅛" across, $85.00. Spooner, crystal w/etch, 5⅞" high, 3¼" across, $95.00. Celery vase, crystal, 7¼" high, 3½" across, $95.00.

Not Shown: Butter dish, crystal w/etch, $110.00. Sugar with lid, crystal, $90.00. Creamer, crystal, $75.00. Spooner, crystal, $85.00. Celery vase, crystal w/etch, $110.00.

Pattern: Atlanta, OMN: No. 228
Manufacturer: Westmoreland Specialty Glass Company
Date Introduced: c. 1905
Colors Made: Crystal
Items/Values: Butter dish, 5⅛" high, 7¾" across,
    $70.00. Sugar with lid (no lid shown), 4¾" across,
    $60.00.
Not Shown: Creamer, $45.00. Spooner, $40.00.

Pattern: Atlas (Northwood), AKA: Concave
    Block
Manufacturer: Northwood Glass Company,
    Wheeling, West Virginia
Date Introduced: c. 1907
Colors Made: Crystal, crystal w/gold,
    maiden's blush (rose)
Items/Values: Butter dish, 6½" high, 7⅜"
    across, $60.00.
Not Shown: Sugar with lid, $50.00. Creamer,
    $40.00. Spooner, $35.00.
Notes: Values for plain crystal pieces are 10%
    less than crystal w/gold pieces. Values given
    are for crystal w/gold pieces.

Pattern: Atlas, AKA: Bullet, Cannon Ball, Crystal Ball, Knobby Bottom

Manufacturer: Bryce Brothers, Pittsburgh, Pennsylvania; U.S. Glass Company, Pittsburgh, Pennsylvania, at factories "A" and "B," c. 1891 – 1904

Date Introduced: c. 1889

Colors Made: Crystal, crystal w/ruby stain (plain or etched)

Items/Values: Butter dish, crystal, 5¾" high, 7" across, $55.00.

Not Shown: Sugar with lid, $55.00. Creamer, $45.00, Spooner, $35.00.

Notes: Some pieces confused with Candlewick pattern by Imperial.

Pattern: Avon

Manufacturer: Bryce Brothers, c. 1885; U.S. Glass Company, Pittsburgh, Pennsylvania, c. 1891

Date Introduced: c. 1885

Colors Made: Crystal/stippled

Items/Values: Butter dish, 3⅝" high, 7" long, $75.00.

Notes: An example of U.S. Glass butter dishes, no known matching pieces.

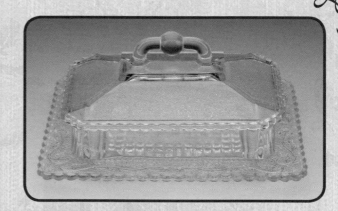

Pattern: Aztec, AKA: New Mexico

Manufacturer: McKee Glass Company, Jeannette, Pennsylvania, c. 1894 – 1915

Date Introduced: c. 1894

Colors Made: Crystal, crystal w/gold, milk white (plain or w/gold)

Reproductions: Butter dish, one and two-piece punch bowls, 5 oz. punch cups, toothpick holder

Items/Values: Butter dish, crystal w/gold, 5¼" high, 7⅜" across, round, $85.00. Sugar with lid, crystal w/gold, 5¾" high, 4⅛" across, scalloped rim, $65.00. Creamer, crystal w/gold, 4⅞" high, 6⅛" across, $55.00. Spooner, crystal w/gold, 3⁹⁄₁₆" high, 3¾" across, $55.00.

Not Shown: Butter dish, crystal w/gold, square, $95.00. Sugar with lid, crystal w/gold, smooth rim, $75.00.

Pattern: Bakewell Ribbon, AKA: Frosted
  Ribbon, Rebecca at the Well, Simple
  Frosted Ribbon
Manufacturer: Bakewell, Pears Company,
  Pittsburgh, Pennsylvania
Date Introduced: c. 1870
Colors Made: Crystal, crystal w/frost
Reproductions: Goblet, footed compote,
  open compote, oblong compote,
  candlesticks
Items/Values: Butter dish, crystal w/frost,
  5⅝" high, 6¼" across, $110.00. Sugar
  with lid, crystal w/frost, 8" high, 4½"
  across, $95.00. Creamer, crystal w/frost,
  5¾" high, 6" across, $75.00. Spooner,
  crystal w/frost, 5¾" high, 3¼" across,
  $60.00. Celery vase, crystal w/frost, 8⅜"
  high, 3¾" across, $90.00.

Pattern: Bakewell Ribbon, AKA: Frosted Ribbon,
  Rebecca at the Well, Simple Frosted Ribbon
Manufacturer: Bakewell, Pears &
  Company, Pittsburgh, Pennsylvania
Date Introduced: c. 1870
Colors Made: Crystal, crystal w/frost
Reproductions: Goblet, footed compote, open
  compote, oblong compote, candlesticks
Items/Values: Creamer, 6" high, 5¾" across,
  $55.00. Spooner, 5¾" high, 3¼" across, $50.00.
Not Shown: Butter dish, $95.00. Sugar with lid,
  $85.00.
Notes: Values given are for plain crystal pieces.

Pattern: Baltimore Pear, OMN: Gypsy. AKA: Double Pear,
  Fig, Maryland Pear, Twin Pear
Manufacturer: Adams & Company, Pittsburgh,
  Pennsylvania; reissued by the U.S. Glass Company at
  factory "A" (Adams & Company), c. 1891
Date Introduced: c. 1874
Colors Made: Crystal
Reproductions: Some from new molds in crystal
Items/Values: Butter dish, 4¾" high, 5⅜" across, $175.00.
Not Shown: Sugar with lid, $110.00. Creamer, $65.00.
  Spooner, $60.00.

Pattern: Bamboo, OMN: LaBelle No. 365. AKA: Bamboo Edge
Manufacturer: Non-flint, LaBelle Glass Company, Bridgeport, Ohio
Date Introduced: c. 1883
Colors Made: Crystal, crystal w/etch
Items/Values: Creamer, 4¾" high, 6¾" across, $90.00.
Not Shown: Butter dish, $165.00. Sugar with lid, $135.00, Spooner, $75.00.
Notes: Values for crystal w/etch pieces are 10% higher than values for plain crystal pieces. Values given are for plain crystal pieces.

Pattern: Banded Star, AKA: Legged Banded Star
Manufacturer: King, Son & Company, Pittsburgh, Pennsylvania
Date Introduced: c. 1880
Colors Made: Crystal
Items/Values: Butter dish, 6¼" high, 5½" across, $100.00. Sugar with lid, 8⅜" high, 4½" across, $85.00. Creamer, 5½" high, 6¼" across, $60.00. Spooner, 5⅛" high, 3½" across, $60.00. Celery vase, 7⅜" high, 4" across, $75.00.

Pattern: Banner
Manufacturer: Bryce Brothers, c. 1885; U.S. Glass Company, Pittsburgh, Pennsylvania, c. 1891
Date Introduced: c. 1885
Colors Made: Amber, blue, crystal
Items/Values: Butter dish, crystal, 3¾" high, 8" long, $130.00.
Notes: An example of U.S. Glass butter dishes, no known matching pieces.

Pattern: Barberry, OMN: Berry, "Seashell"

Manufacturer: McKee & Brothers, Pittsburgh, Pennsylvania,
  c. 1880; The Boston & Sandwich Glass Company,
  Sandwich, Massachusetts, c. 1850 – 1860s

Date Introduced: c. 1850

Colors Made: Crystal

Items/Values: Butter dish, design on rim, $210.00.

Not Shown: Butter dish, plain rim, $95.00. Sugar with lid,
  $95.00. Creamer, $95.00. Spooner, $70.00.

Pattern: Barley

Manufacturer: Unknown

Date Introduced: Unknown

Colors Made: Crystal, any color is rare

Items/Values: Creamer, crystal, 5⅜" high, 5"
  across, $35.00.

Not Shown: Butter dish, $60.00. Sugar with
  lid, $50.00. Spooner, $30.00.

Pattern: Batesville
Manufacturer: Unknown
Date Introduced: c. 1875 – 1885
Colors Made: Crystal, crystal w/etch
Items/Values: Sugar with lid (no lid shown),
   5" across, $80.00. Celery vase, 7" high,
   4¼" across, $75.00.
Not Shown: Butter dish, $95.00. Creamer,
   $65.00. Spooner, $50.00.
Notes: Values for crystal w/etch pieces are
   10% more than plain crystal. Values given
   are for crystal w/etch pieces.

Pattern: Bead and Scroll
Manufacturer: U. S. Glass Company
Date Introduced: c. 1901
Colors Made: Cobalt, crystal, crystal
   w/gold, emerald w/ruby stain
Items/Values: Butter dish, crystal
   w/gold, 5½" high, 7⅜" across,
   $85.00. Sugar with lid, crystal
   w/gold, 6⅜" high, 4" across,
   $75.00. Creamer, crystal w/gold,
   4⅝" high, 5¼" across, $60.00.
   Spooner, crystal w/gold, 4³⁄₁₆"
   high, 3¾" across, $60.00.

Pattern: Bead Column
Manufacturer: Kokomo Glass Company
Date Introduced: c. 1905
Colors Made: Crystal
Items/Values: Butter dish, 5¾" high,
   7¼" across, $65.00. Creamer, 4¾"
   high, 5¼" across, $40.00. Spooner,
   4¼" high, 3⅜" across, $35.00.
Not Shown: Sugar with lid, $55.00.

Pattern: Bead Swag, OMN: No. 1295
Manufacturer: A.H. Heisey & Company, Newark, Ohio
Date Introduced: c. 1899
Colors Made: Crystal, opal, ruby stain (w/gold or decoration)
Items/Values: Butter dish, opal with gold trim, painted rose, 5⅝"
   high, 7¼" across, $110.00.
Not Shown: Sugar with lid, $100.00. Creamer, $80.00.
   Spooner, $75.00.

Pattern: Beaded Acorn
   Medallion, AKA: Beaded Acorn
Manufacturer: Boston Silver
   Glass Company, East
   Cambridge, Massachusetts, c.
   1869; also attributed to Boston
   & Sandwich Glass Company,
   Sandwich, Massachusetts,
   based on shards at the factory
   site
Date Introduced: c. 1869
Colors Made: Crystal
Items/Values: Butter dish, 4¼"
   high, 5¹³⁄₁₆" across, $125.00.
   Sugar with lid, 7¼" high, 4¹⁄₁₆"
   across, $95.00. Spooner, 5⅜"
   high, 3⅜" across, $50.00.
Not Shown: Creamer, $80.00.

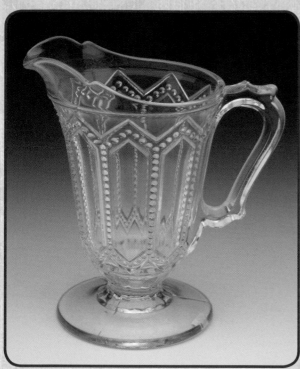

Pattern: Beaded Arch Panels, AKA: Beaded Arch, Archaic Gothic
Manufacturer: Burlington Glass Works, Canada
Date Introduced: c. 1890
Colors Made: Crystal
Items/Values: Creamer, 5¼" high, 5⅛" across, $40.00.
Not Shown: Butter dish, $60.00. Sugar with lid, $50.00. Spooner, $35.00.

Pattern: Beaded Dart Band, OMN: Duncan No. 600. AKA: Beaded Diamond Band
Manufacturer: George Duncan & Sons, c. 1882; U.S. Glass Company, c. 1891
Date Introduced: c. 1882
Colors Made: Crystal
Items/Values: Butter dish, 5⅛" high, 7" across, $55.00.
Not Shown: Sugar with lid, $50.00. Creamer, $40.00. Spooner, $35.00.

Pattern: Beaded Grape Medallion
Manufacturer: The Boston Silver Glass Company, East Cambridge, Massachusetts, c. 1869; attributed to the Boston & Sandwich Glass Company, Sandwich, Massachusetts, based on shards found at the factory site
Date Introduced: c. 1869
Colors Made: Crystal
Reproductions: Goblet (crystal, crystal w/stain, colors) marked with "R" in shield on base
Items/Values: Sugar with lid (no lid shown), 4" across, $90.00. Spooner, 5⅛" high, 3½" across, $40.00.
Not Shown: Butter dish, $100.00. Creamer, $70.00.

Pattern: Beaded Mirror, AKA: Beaded Medallion
Manufacturer: Boston Silver Glass Company, East Cambridge,
   Massachusetts, c. 1869; attributed to the Boston & Sandwich
   Glass Company, Sandwich, Massachusetts, based on shards
   found at the factory site
Date Introduced: c. 1869
Colors Made: Crystal
Items/Values: Spooner, 5½" high, 3⅜" across, $40.00.
Not Shown: Butter dish, $100.00. Sugar with lid, $80.00.
   Creamer, $70.00.

Pattern: Beaded Oval & Scroll, AKA: Dot
Manufacturer: Bryce McKee & Company
Date Introduced: c. 1880
Colors Made: Crystal
Items/Values: Butter dish, 4¾" high, 6¼" across, $65.00. Creamer, 4⁷⁄₁₆"
   high, 4½" across, $50.00. Spooner, 4¼" high, 3½" across, $50.00.
Not Shown: Sugar with lid, $50.00.

Pattern: Beaded Panel & Sunburst, OMN: No. 1235
Manufacturer: A.H. Heisey Glass Company, Newark, Ohio, discontinued before 1913
Date Introduced: c. 1897
Colors Made: Crystal, crystal w/amber
Items/Values: Butter dish, crystal, 6¼" high, 8⅝" across, $135.00.
Not Shown: Sugar with lid, $100.00. Creamer, $60.00. Spooner, $55.00.

Pattern: Beaded Swirl, OMN: George Duncan No. 335. AKA: Swirled Column
Manufacturer: George Duncan & Sons, Pittsburgh, Pennsylvania; U.S. Glass Company, Pittsburgh, Pennsylvania, after 1891
Date Introduced: c. 1890
Colors Made: Crystal, emerald (plain or w/gold)
Items/Values: Butter dish, footed, 6½" high, 8¼" across, $90.00.
Not Shown: Butter dish, flat, $75.00. Sugar with lid, flat, $50.00. Sugar with lid, footed, $75.00. Creamer, flat, $50.00. Creamer, footed, $70.00. Spooner, flat, $50.00. Spooner, footed, $70.00.
Notes: Values for crystal pieces are 25% less than other colors. Values given are for emerald pieces.

Pattern: Beaded Swirl and Disc, AKA: U.S. Glass No. 15085
Manufacturer: U.S. Glass Company
Date Introduced: c. 1904
Colors Made: Crystal, crystal w/blue, crystal w/green, crystal w/yellow stain
Items/Values: Butter dish, crystal, 5³⁄₁₆" high, 7" across, $75.00. Creamer, crystal, 4" high, 4½" across, $50.00. Spooner, crystal, 3⅞" high, 3¼" across, $60.00.
Not Shown: Sugar with lid, $60.00.

Pattern: Belmont No. 100, AKA: Daisy and Button
 Plain, Daisy and Button Scalloped Edge
Manufacturer: Belmont Glass Works, Bellaire, Ohio
Date Introduced: c. 1886
Colors Made: Amber, canary, crystal
Items/Values: Butter dish, amber, 8⅜" high, 8" across,
 $195.00.
Not Shown: Sugar with lid, $150.00. Creamer, $135.00.
 Spooner, $145.00.
Notes: Values for plain crystal pieces are 50% less than
 other pieces. Values given are for amber pieces.

Pattern: Bethlehem Star, AKA: Bright Star, Six Point Star, Star Burst
Manufacturer: Indiana Glass Company, Dunkirk, Indiana; Jefferson Glass Company,
 Toronto, Montreal, Canada
Date Introduced: c. 1912
Colors Made: Crystal
Items/Values: Butter dish, 5¾" high, 7¼" across, $95.00. Sugar with lid, 3⅝" high, 7"
 across handle to handle, $80.00. Creamer, 4⅝" high, 5½" across, $60.00. Spooner, 4³⁄₁₆"
 high, 6" across, $60.00.

Pattern: Beveled Diamond & Star, AKA: Diamond Prisms, Albany
Manufacturer: Tarentum Glass Company, Tarentum, Pennsylvania, 1894 – 1918, burned in 1918
Date Introduced: c. 1894
Colors Made: Crystal, crystal w/ruby stain
Items/Values: Butter dish, crystal, 5⅜" across, 7⅜" across, $85.00. Sugar with lid, crystal, 7⅛" high, 4⅛" across, $80.00. Creamer, crystal, 5¼" high, 5" across, $65.00. Spooner, crystal, 5" high, 3¾" across, $50.00. Celery vase, crystal, 6½" high, 4⅛" across, $70.00.

Pattern: Bird and Strawberry, OMN: Indiana Glass No.157. AKA: Blue Bird, Flying Bird and Stawberry, Strawberry and Bird
Manufacturer: Indiana Glass Company, Dunkirk, Indiana
Date Introduced: c. 1914
Colors Made: Crystal, crystal w/decoration
Reproductions: Oval relish tray (clear, blue), covered compote (clear, pale green)
Items/Values: Butter dish, crystal w/blue, red, and green stain, 5⅝" high, 7⅜" across, $350.00.
Not Shown: Sugar with lid, $300.00. Creamer, $225.00. Spooner, $250.00.
Notes: Values for plain crystal pieces are 50% less than crystal w/decoration. Values given are for crystal w/decoration pieces.

Pattern: Blazing Cornucopia, AKA: Paisley, Paisley with Dots
Manufacturer: U.S. Glass Company
Date Introduced: c. 1913
Colors Made: Amethyst w/stain, crystal, crystal w/gold, green w/stain, red w/stain
Items/Values: Butter dish, crystal with gold, 5⅝" high, 7⅞" across, $110.00.
Not Shown: Sugar with lid, crystal w/gold, $95.00. Creamer, crystal w/gold, $80.00. Spooner, crystal w/gold, $65.00.

Pattern: Bleeding Heart, OMN: King's Floral Ware, U.S. Glass No. 85 – New Floral
Manufacturer: King, Son & Company, Pittsburgh, Pennsylvania, c. 1875; Specialty Glass Company, c. 1888
Date Introduced: c. 1875
Colors Made: Crystal, milk
Items/Values: Butter dish, crystal, lid only shown, $150.00. Sugar with lid, two styles, no lids shown, 4" across, crystal, $135.00 each style.
Not Shown: Creamer, flat, pressed handle, $65.00. Creamer, footed, applied handle, $110.00. Spooner, crystal, 5⁹⁄₁₆" high, 3⅛" across, $65.00.

Pattern: Block and Circle, OMN: Mellor
Manufacturer: Gillinder & Sons, Philadelphia, Pennsylvania
Date Introduced: c. 1874
Colors Made: Crystal
Items/Values: Celery vase, 8⅜" high, 4¼" across, $55.00.
Not Shown: Butter dish, $65.00. Sugar with lid, $55.00. Creamer, $40.00. Spooner, $40.00.

Pattern: Block and Fan
Manufacturer: Richards & Hartley, Tarentum,
   Pennsylvania, c. 1885; U.S. Glass Company,
   Pittsburgh, Pennsylvania at factory "E," after 1891
Date Introduced: c. 1885
Colors Made: Crystal, crystal w/ruby stain
Items/Values: Celery vase, 7" high, $50.00.
Not Shown: Butter dish, $80.00. Sugar with lid,
   $65.00. Creamer, $50.00. Spooner, $40.00.

Pattern: Block and Lattice, AKA: Big Button, Red Block and
   Lattice, Block and Star, Pioneer No. 9
Manufacturer: Pioneer Glass Company
Date Introduced: c. 1891
Colors Made: Crystal, crystal w/amber, crystal w/ruby stain
Items/Values: Butter dish, crystal w/ruby stain, 5¾" high,
   7½" across, $125.00. Creamer, crystal w/ruby stain, 4½"
   high, 4⅞" across, $100.00. Spooner, crystal w/ruby stain,
   4⅝" high, 3¼" across, $85.00.
Not Shown: Butter dish, crystal w/amber band, $100.00.
   Sugar with lid, crystal w/amber, $110.00. Sugar with lid,
   crystal w/ruby stain, $140.00. Creamer, crystal w/amber,
   $85.00. Spooner, crystal w/amber, $70.00.

Pattern: Block and Lattice, AKA: Big Button, Red Block and Lattice, Block and Star, Pioneer No. 9
Manufacturer: Pioneer Glass Company
Date Introduced: c. 1891
Colors Made: Crystal, crystal w/amber, crystal w/ruby stain
Items/Values: Butter dish, crystal w/amber, 5¾" high, 7½" across, $100.00. Sugar with lid, crystal w/amber, 8" high,
   4½" across, $110.00.
Not Shown: Butter dish, crystal w/ruby stain, $125.00. Sugar with lid, crystal w/ruby stain, $140.00. Creamer, crystal
   w/amber, $85.00. Creamer, crystal w/ruby stain, $100.00. Spooner, crystal w/amber, $70.00. Spooner, crystal
   w/ruby stain, $85.00.

Pattern: Block and Pleat, OMN: Persian. AKA: Three Stories,
    Small Block and Prism
Manufacturer: Bryce, Higbee and Company
Date Introduced: c. 1885
Colors Made: Crystal
Items/Values: Creamer, 5¾" high, 5½" across, $45.00. Celery
    vase, 7¼" high, 4½" across, $50.00.
Not Shown: Butter dish, $60.00. Sugar with lid, $50.00.
    Spooner, $30.00.

Pattern: Bordered Ellipse, OMN: McKee's No. 79
Manufacturer: McKee & Brothers (National Glass), Jeannette, Pennsylvania
Date Introduced: c. 1902
Colors Made: Crystal, crystal w/ruby stain
Items/Values: Butter dish, crystal, 5½" high, 7⅜" across, $70.00. Sugar with lid
    (no lid shown), crystal, 4" across, $55.00.
Not Shown: Creamer, $40.00. Spooner, $35.00.

OUR ZENITH RUBY AND GOLD DECORATED DINING SET ASSORTMENT

Pattern: Bosc Pear
Manufacturer: Indiana Glass Company
Date Introduced: c. 1913
Colors Made: Crystal, flash pears, gold, purple
Items/Values: Butter dish, $95.00. Sugar with lid, $80.00.
  Creamer, $75.00. Spooner, $60.00.
Notes: Values for plain crystal pieces are 20% less than
  crystal w/ruby decorated/gold. Values given are for
  crystal w/ruby decorated/gold.

Pattern: Bow Tie, OMN: Thompson No. 18. AKA: American Bow Tie
Manufacturer: Thompson Glass Company, Uniontown, Pennsylvania
Date Introduced: c. 1889
Colors Made: Crystal
Items/Values: Butter dish, 5⅝" high, 6⅝" across, $175.00. Sugar with lid, 7⅞" high, 4⅛" across, $150.00. Creamer, 5¼" high, 5¹⁄₁₆" across, $75.00. Spooner, 4¾" high, 3⅜" across, $85.00.

Pattern: Britannic
Manufacturer: McKee & Brothers Glass Works (under National Glass Company), Pittsburgh, Pennsylvania, c. 1894 until sometime after 1903
Date Introduced: c. 1894
Colors Made: Crystal, crystal w/amber, crystal w/ruby (emerald or other colors rare)
Items/Values: Creamer, crystal, 4¼" high, 5³⁄₁₆" across, $50.00.
Not Shown: Butter dish, $85.00. Sugar with lid, $65.00. Spooner, $40.00.

Pattern: Bryce Fashion
Manufacturer: Bryce Brothers, c. 1880s; U.S. Glass Company, c. 1891
Date Introduced: c. 1880s
Colors Made: Amber, blue, canary, crystal
Items/Values: Butter dish, 5" high, 7⅝" across, $160.00.
Notes: An example of U.S. Glass Company's special butter dishes, no known matching pieces.

Pattern: Buckle with Star, OMN: Orient. AKA: Buckle and Star, Late Buckle and Star

Manufacturer: Bryce Brothers, c. 1880s; U.S. Glass Company, c. 1891

Date Introduced: c. 1880s

Colors Made: Crystal

Items/Values: Butter dish, 5¼" high, 6⅛" across, unusual finial, $80.00. Creamer, 6⅜" high, 5¹¹⁄₁₆" across, $50.00. Spooner, 6⅛" high, 3⅞" across, $40.00.

Not Shown: Sugar with lid, $70.00.

Pattern: Buckle, Early, OMN: Gillinder No. 15

Manufacturer: Unknown, often attributed to Gillinder & Sons, Pittsburgh, Pennsylvania, c. late 1870s; also Boston & Sandwich Glass Company, Sandwich, Massachusetts, and Union Glass Company, Somerville, Massachusetts, based on shards found at each factory site

Date Introduced: c. late 1870s

Colors Made: Crystal

Items/Values: Sugar with lid (no lid shown), non-flint, $65.00.

Not Shown: Butter dish, flint, $125.00. Butter dish, non-flint, $60.00. Sugar with lid, flint, $125.00. Creamer, flint, $95.00. Creamer, non-flint, $65.00. Spooner, flint, $60.00. Spooner, non-flint, $40.00.

Pattern: Bull's Eye and Daisy, OMN: U.S. Glass No. 15117 – Newport. AKA: Knobby Bull's Eye

Manufacturer: U.S. Glass Company, Pittsburgh, Pennsylvania, at factory "F" and factory "P"

Date Introduced: c. 1909

Colors Made: Crystal, crystal w/amethyst stain, crystal w/green stain, crystal w/pink stain, crystal w/ruby stain (plain or w/gold)

Reproductions: Goblet, 9 oz. swing footed vase (amber, blue, canary yellow, milk white, and sapphire)

Items/Values: Butter dish, crystal w/gold and green, 5" high, 8¼" across, $125.00. Sugar with lid, crystal w/gold and green, $85.00. Creamer, crystal w/gold and green, 4⅝" high, 6" across, $70.00. Spooner, crystal w/gold and green, 4⅜" high, 7" across, $65.00.

Pattern: Bull's Eye and Fan, OMN: U.S. Glass No. 15090, AKA: Daisies in Oval Panels

Manufacturer: U.S. Glass Company, Pittsburgh, Pennsylvania

Date Introduced: c. 1904

Colors Made: Amethyst stain, blue, crystal, green, pink

Items/Values: Butter dish, 6" high, 7⅞" across, $75.00.

Not Shown: Sugar with lid, $80.00. Creamer, $70.00, Spooner, $45.00.

Notes: Values for plain crystal pieces are 10% less than crystal w/gold pieces. Values given are for crystal w/gold pieces.

Pattern: Bullet Emblem, AKA: Bullet, Eagle and Shield, Eagle and Arms, Emblem, Shield
Manufacturer: U.S. Glass Company, Pittsburgh, Pennsylvania
Date Introduced: c. 1898
Colors Made: Crystal, crystal w/decoration
Items/Values: Butter dish (lid only shown), crystal, $425.00. Sugar with lid (no lid shown), crystal, 4½" across, $340.00.
Not Shown: Creamer, crystal, $215.00. Spooner, crystal, $190.00.

Pattern: Button Arches, OMN: Duncan No. 39, AKA: Scalloped Diamond, Scalloped Diamond – Red Top, Scalloped Daisy – Red Top
Manufacturer: George Duncan Sons & Company, Washington, Pennsylvania, c. 1897; Duncan & Miller Glass Company, c. 1900
Date Introduced: c. 1897
Colors Made: Crystal, crystal w/gold (plain or w/decoration), crystal w/ruby stain, white clambroth
Reproductions: Some in crystal and crystal w/ruby stain by Westlake Ruby Glassworks
Items/Values: Butter dish, crystal w/gold, 5¾" high, 7⅝" across, $85.00. Sugar with lid, crystal w/gold, 6⅝" high, 3⅞" across, $65.00. Creamer, crystal w/gold, 4⅛" high, 4⅞" across, $60.00. Spooner, crystal w/gold, 3¾" high, 3⅛" across, $40.00. Toothpick holder, crystal w/decoration, 2¼" high, 1⅞" across, $25.00.
Not Shown: Butter dish, crystal, $75.00. Sugar with lid, crystal, $60.00. Creamer, crystal, $55.00. Spooner, crystal, $35.00. Toothpick holder, crystal w/gold, $30.00.

Pattern: Button Panel, OMN: No. 44.
AKA: Diamond Crystal, Rainbow
Variant
Manufacturer: George Duncan &
Sons, Pittsburgh, Pennsylvania
Date Introduced: c. 1900
Colors Made: Crystal, crystal w/gold,
crystal w/ruby stain
Items/Values: Butter dish, 5⅝" high,
8" across, $95.00. Sugar with lid,
6⅝" high, 4⅝" across, $85.00.
Creamer, 4⅜" high, 5⅛" across,
$70.00. Spooner, 4⅛" high, 3½"
across, $65.00.
Notes: Values for plain crystal pieces
are 10% less than values for other
pieces. Values given are for crystal
w/gold pieces.

Pattern: Buzz Star, OMN: U.S. Glass No. 15101.
AKA: Whirligig, Comet
Manufacturer: U.S. Glass Company
Date Introduced: c. 1907
Colors Made: Crystal
Items/Values: Butter dish, lid only shown,
$55.00.
Not Shown: Sugar with lid, $45.00. Creamer,
$30.00. Spooner, $30.00.

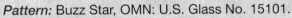

Pattern: California, OMN: U.S. Glass No
15059, Beaded Grape. AKA: Beaded
Grape and Vine, Grape and Vine
Manufacturer: U.S. Glass Company,
Pittsburgh, Pennsylvania
Date Introduced: c. 1899
Colors Made: Crystal, emerald w/gold
Reproductions: Many, in colors and
crystal
Items/Values: Sugar with lid (no lid
shown), crystal, 3¾" across, $80.00.
Creamer, crystal, 3¼" high, 5¾"
across, $45.00.
Not Shown: Butter dish, crystal, $110.00.
Spooner, crystal, $45.00.

Pattern: Cambridge No. 2504, OMN: Robinson No. 129. AKA: Josephine's Fan

Manufacturer: Robinson Glass Company, c. 1896; Cambridge Glass Company, Cambridge, Ohio, c. 1903

Date Introduced: c. 1896

Colors Made: Crystal

Items/Values: Packers's butter dish, ¼ lb., 4¼" high, 5⅜" across, $100.00. Cruet, 5⅛" high, $80.00.

Not Shown: Butter dish, plain, $80.00. Sugar with lid, $65.00. Creamer, $40.00. Spooner, $40.00.

Pattern: Cambridge No. 2692, AKA: Near Cut No. 2692, Guernsey Near Cut

Manufacturer: Cambridge Glass Company

Date Introduced: c. 1908

Colors Made: Crystal, crystal w/rose blush

Items/Values: Creamer, 4¾" high, $50.00.

Not Shown: Butter dish, $85.00. Sugar with lid, $75.00. Spooner, $50.00.

Notes: Values for plain crystal pieces are 30% less than other pieces. Values given are for crystal w/rose blush.

Pattern: Cambridge No. 2760, AKA: Red Sunflower, Near Cut No. 2760, Near Cut Daisy

Manufacturer: Cambridge Glass Company

Date Introduced: c. 1910

Colors Made: Crystal, crystal w/gold, crystal w/ruby stain

Items/Value: Individual sugar, missing lid, value with lid, $50.00.

Not Shown: Butter dish, $80.00. Sugar with lid, $65.00. Creamer, $50.00. Spooner, $45.00.

Notes: Values given are for plain crystal pieces. Add 100% for crystal w/ruby stain.

Pattern: Cambridge Buzz Saw, OMN: Near Cut No. 2699
Manufacturer: Cambridge Glass Company, Cambridge, Ohio
Date Introduced: c. 1907
Colors Made: Crystal
Items/Values: Butter dish, 5⅜" high, 7¼" across, $65.00.
Not Shown: Sugar with lid, $50.00. Creamer, $40.00. Spooner, $30.00.

Pattern: Cane Horseshoe, OMN: Paragon. AKA: U.S. Glass No. 15118
Manufacturer: U.S. Glass Company, Pittsburgh, Pennsylvania, factory "F," Ripley & Company
Date Introduced: c. 1909
Colors Made: Crystal, crystal w/gold
Items/Values: Butter dish, crystal, 5" high, 7⅜" across, $75.00. Sugar with lid, crystal, 6½" high, 7⅛" across, $50.00.
Not Shown: Creamer, $35.00. Spooner, $25.00.

Pattern: Cane Insert, AKA: Arched Cane & Fan
Manufacturer: Tarentum Glass Company
Date Introduced: c. 1898
Colors Made: Crystal, crystal w/gold
Items/Values: Butter dish, crystal w/gold, 5⅞" high, 7¼" across, $60.00.
Not Shown: Sugar with lid, crystal w/gold, $50.00. Creamer, crystal w/gold, $40.00. Spooner, crystal w/gold, $35.00.

Pattern: Cannonball Pinwheel, OMN: U.S. Glass No. 15094. AKA: Caldonia, Pinwheel

Manufacturer: U.S. Glass Company, 1906; Federal Glass, 1914

Date Introduced: c. 1906

Colors Made: Crystal

Items/Values: Butter dish, 5" high, 7½" across, $90.00. Sugar with lid, 6½" high, 4" across, $85.00. Creamer, 3⅝" high, 5¾" across, $70.00. Spooner, 3⅝" high, 3¾" across, $50.00.

Pattern: Cardinal, AKA: Blue Jay, Cardinal Bird

Manufacturer: Ohio Flint Glass Company, Lancaster, Ohio

Date Introduced: c. 1875

Colors Made: Crystal

Reproductions: Creamer and goblet in blue, green, and crystal, by L.G. Wright and Summit Art Glass Company, unmarked

Items/Values: Butter dish, 4⅜" high, 5⅞" across, $150.00. Sugar with lid, 7¼" high, 4¼" across, $130.00. Creamer, 5¾" high, 5¼" across, $85.00. Spooner, 5¹⁄₁₆" high, 3⅜" across, $90.00.

Pattern: Carmen, OMN: No. 575 Fostoria Glass. AKA: Panelled Diamonds and Finecut
Manufacturer: Fostoria Glass Company, Moundsville, West Virginia
Date Introduced: c. 1896
Colors Made: Crystal, crystal w/amber stain, crystal w/etch
Items/Values: Butter dish, crystal, $5\frac{7}{8}$" high, $7\frac{3}{4}$" across, $95.00. Creamer, crystal, $4\frac{7}{8}$" high, $5\frac{3}{16}$" across, $65.00.
Not Shown: Sugar with lid, $80.00. Spooner, $50.00.

Pattern: Carolina, AKA: Inverness, Mayflower, No. 15083
Manufacturer: Originally issued in 1890 by Bryce Brothers in Pittsburgh, Pennsylvania. In 1903, two years after Bryce became a member of the U.S. Glass Company, it was reissued as a state pattern.
Date Introduced: c. 1890
Colors Made: Crystal, crystal w/enamel, crystal w/frost, ruby or purple stain souvenirs
Items/Values: Butter dish, crystal, $5\frac{1}{4}$" high, 7" across, $80.00. Creamer, crystal, $5\frac{1}{4}$" high, $5\frac{1}{2}$" across, $50.00. Spooner, crystal, 5" high, 4" across, $45.00.
Not Shown: Sugar with lid, crystal, $65.00.

Pattern: Cathedral, OMN: Orion. AKA: Waffle and Fine Cut
Manufacturer: Bryce Brothers, Pittsburgh, Pennsylvania; U.S. Glass Company, Pittsburgh, Pennsylvania, after 1891
Date Introduced: c. 1885
Colors Made: Amber, amethyst, blue, crystal, ruby stain, vaseline
Items/Values: Butter dish, $5\frac{1}{2}$" high, $7\frac{1}{4}$" across, $75.00. Sugar with lid, crystal, $8\frac{5}{8}$" high, 4" across, $90.00. Creamer, footed, crystal, $6\frac{3}{8}$" high, 5" across, $55.00. Spooner, crystal, $5\frac{3}{4}$" high, $3\frac{1}{2}$" across, $55.00.

Pattern: Celtic, OMN: No. 100
Manufacturer: New Martinsville Glass Manufacturing Company, New Martinsville, West Virginia
Date Introduced: c. 1903
Colors Made: Crystal, crystal w/gold
Items/Values: Butter dish (lid only shown), crystal w/gold trim, $55.00.
Not Shown: Sugar with lid, $45.00. Creamer, $35.00. Spooner, $35.00.
Notes: Values for plain crystal pieces are 10% less than pieces with gold. Values given are for crystal w/gold pieces.

Pattern: Chain
Manufacturer: Unknown
Date Introduced: c. 1870s
Colors Made: Crystal
Items/Values: Creamer, 6" high, 6" across, $35.00. Spooner, 5½" high, 3⅝" across, $30.00.
Not Shown: Butter dish, $60.00. Sugar with lid, $50.00.

Pattern: Chain with Star, OMN: Bryce No. 79. AKA: Chain, Frosted Chain
Manufacturer: Bryce Brothers, Pittsburgh, Pennsylvania, c.1882; U.S. Glass Company, Pittsburgh, Pennsylvania, c. 1891
Date Introduced: c. 1882
Colors Made: Crystal
Items/Values: Butter dish, 4½" high, 6" across, $85.00. Sugar with lid (no lid shown), 5" across, $85.00. Creamer, 5½" high, 5¼" across, $65.00. Spooner, 5³⁄₁₆" high, 3¾" across, $60.00.

Pattern: Champion, AKA: Seagrit, Fan with Crossbars, Greentown No. 11, Diamond and Long Sunburst

Manufacturer: Indiana Tumbler & Goblet Company, c. 1894; McKee Brothers, c. 1896; Indiana Glass Company, c. 1904

Date Introduced: c. 1894

Colors Made: Crystal, crystal w/amber stain, crystal w/gold, crystal w/ruby stain

Items/Values: Butter dish, crystal w/gold, 5½" high, 7⅞" across, $90.00. Sugar with lid, crystal w/gold, 7⅛" high, 4" across, $70.00. Creamer, crystal w/gold, 4⅞" high, 5" across, $70.00. Spooner, crystal w/gold, 4¾" high, 3⅝" across, $55.00. Celery vase, crystal, 5⅞" high, 4¼" across, $60.00.

Not Shown: Butter dish, crystal, $80.00. Sugar with lid, crystal, $60.00. Creamer, crystal, $60.00. Spooner, crystal, $50.00. Celery vase, crystal w/gold, $70.00.

Pattern: Chandelier, OMN: O'Hara No. 82 – Crown Jewels

Manufacturer: O'Hara Glass Company, Pittsburgh, Pennsylvania, c. 1888; U.S. Glass Company, Pittsburgh, Pennsylvania, at factory "L" after the 1891 merger

Date Introduced: c. 1888

Colors Made: Crystal, crystal w/etch

Items/Values: Creamer, crystal, 4⅝" high, 4¾" across, $75.00. Spooner, crystal, 4¾" high, 4⅛" across, $60.00. Celery vase, crystal, 6⅛" high, 4" across, $75.00.

Not Shown: Butter dish, $125.00. Sugar with lid, $110.00.

Pattern: Cherry Thumbprint, AKA: Cherry and Gable, Paneled Cherry
Manufacturer: H. Northwood Company, Wheeling, West Virginia, c. 1904; Westmoreland Glass Company, Grapeville, Pennsylvania, 1907
Date Introduced: c. 1904
Colors Made: Crystal, crystal w/color stain (plain or w/gold)
Items/Values: Butter dish, crystal trimmed in gold and ruby, 6" high, 7¾" across, $125.00.
Not Shown: Sugar with lid, $90.00. Creamer, $75.00. Spooner, $75.00.

Pattern: Chesterfield, AKA: Diamond Lattice, No. 2500 Cambridge
Manufacturer: Cambridge Glass Company, Cambridge, Ohio
Date Introduced: c. 1903
Colors Made: Crystal
Items/Values: Butter dish, 6⅞" high, 7½" across, $40.00.
Not Shown: Sugar with lid, $35.00. Creamer, $30.00. Spooner, $30.00.

Pattern: Church Windows, AKA: Tulip Petals, Columbia
Manufacturer: U.S. Glass Company No. 15082 (King, Richards & Hartley) made at factories "K" and "E." King located in Pittsburgh; Richards & Hartley located in Tarentum, Pennsylvania
Date Introduced: c. 1903
Colors Made: Amber stain, crystal, crystal w/gold, rose blush

Items/Values: Butter dish, crystal w/gold trim, 5¹¹⁄₁₆" high, 8⅛" across, $55.00. Creamer, crystal, 4⅞" high, 5¾" across, $35.00.
Not Shown: Butter dish, crystal, $50.00. Sugar with lid, crystal, $45.00. Sugar with lid, crystal w/gold, $50.00. Creamer, crystal w/gold, $40.00. Spooner, crystal, $35.00. Spooner, crystal w/gold, $40.00.

Pattern: Classic
Manufacturer: Gillinder & Sons, Philadelphia, Pennsylvania
Date Introduced: c. 1875
Colors Made: Crystal w/frost
Items/Values: Butter dish, 6⅞" high, 6½" across, $375.00. Sugar with lid, 8⅛" high, 5" across, $280.00. Creamer, 5¾" high, 5¾" across, $150.00. Spooner, 5⅛" high, 3¼" across, $120.00. Milk pitcher, 1 qt., 8¾" high, 7¾" across, $925.00.
Notes: All of these pieces have log feet and collared bases.

Pattern: Classic Medallion, AKA: Cameo
Manufacturer: Richards & Hartley Glass Company, Tarentum, Pennsylvania
Date Introduced: c. 1870
Colors Made: Crystal
Items/Values: Sugar with lid (no lid shown), 4" across, $90.00. Creamer, 5¾" high, 5⅝" across, $45.00.
Not Shown: Butter dish, $120.00. Spooner, $35.00.
Notes: Conventional or tiny lion finial.

Pattern: Clear Diagonal Band, AKA: California State
Manufacturer: Unknown
Date Introduced: c. 1880s
Colors Made: Crystal
Items/Values: Butter dish, 4⅞" high, 6½" across, $70.00. Sugar with lid (no lid shown), 4⁹⁄₁₆" across, $65.00. Creamer, 5¾" high, 5½" across, $50.00. Spooner, 5⅜" high, 3¾" across, $45.00. Celery vase, 8½" high, 4⅛" across, $50.00.

Pattern: Clio, AKA: Daisy Button & Almond Band
Manufacturer: Challinor, Taylor & Company
Date Introduced: c. 1885
Colors Made: Blue, canary, crystal, green
Items/Values: Butter dish, crystal, 6⅜" high, 6⅞" across, $75.00. Creamer, crystal, 4½" high, 5¾" across, $45.00.
Not Shown: Sugar with lid, $60.00. Spooner, $35.00.

Pattern: Co-Op No. 276, OMN: No. 276
Manufacturer: Co-Operative Flint Glass Company, Beaver Falls, Pennsylvania
Date Introduced: c. 1900
Colors Made: Crystal, crystal w/gold
Items/Values: Butter dish, 5½" high, 7¾" across, $80.00. Sugar with lid, 6"
   high, 5" across, $65.00. Creamer, 5½" high, 5¾" across, $50.00. Spooner,
   3¾" high, 3¾" across, $50.00.
Notes: Values for plain crystal pieces are 10% less than crystal w/gold. Values
   given are for crystal w/gold pieces.

Pattern: Coarse Zig-Zag, AKA: Highland
Manufacturer: J.B. Higbee Glass Company,
   c. 1908; New Martinsville Glass
   Manufacturing Company, c. 1917
Date Introduced: c. 1908
Colors Made: Crystal
Items/Values: Creamer, 4⅞" high, 5⅛"
   across, $30.00. Spooner, 4⅞" high,
   3½" across, $30.00.
Not Shown: Butter dish, $45.00. Sugar with
   lid, $35.00.

Pattern: Colonial, AKA: Estelle, Paden City No. 205
Manufacturer: J.B. Higbee Glass Company, 1910;
   Paden City Glass Manufacturing Company, 1919
Date Introduced: c. 1910
Colors Made: Crystal
Items/Values: Butter dish, 5½" high, 8" across,
   $50.00.
Not Shown: Sugar with lid, $40.00. Creamer, $35.00.
   Spooner, $30.00.

Pattern: Colonis, OMN: U.S. Glass No. 15145
Manufacturer: U.S. Glass Company, Glassport, Pennsylvania, factory "O" - GP
Date Introduced: c. 1913
Colors Made: Crystal, crystal w/gold
Items/Values: Butter dish, crystal w/gold, 5¼" high, 7¼" across, $85.00. Sugar with lid,
   crystal w/gold, 6" high, 6½" across, $75.00. Creamer, crystal w/gold, 3½" high, 5½"
   across, $50.00. Spooner, crystal w/gold, 4" high, 6" across, $45.00.
Notes: Values for plain crystal pieces are 10% less than crystal w/gold. Values given are
   for crystal w/gold pieces.

Pattern: Colorado, OMN: U.S. Glass No. 15057 – Colorado. AKA: Jewel, Lacy Jewel

Manufacturer: U.S. Glass Company, Pittsburgh, Pennsylvania, c. 1899 to about 1920

Date Introduced: c. 1899

Colors Made: Blue, crystal, green

Items/Values: Butter dish, crystal, 6½" high, 6¾" across, $70.00.

Not Shown: Sugar with lid, crystal, $65.00. Creamer, crystal, $50.00. Spooner, crystal, $50.00.

Pattern: Colorado, OMN: U.S. Glass No. 15057 – Colorado. AKA: Jewel, Lacy Jewel

Manufacturer: U.S. Glass Company, Pittsburgh, Pennsylvania, c. 1899 to about 1920

Date Introduced: c. 1899

Colors Made: Blue, crystal, emerald (plain or w/gold)

Reproductions: Toothpick in blue, crystal, or green

Items/Values: Butter dish, emerald w/gold trim, 6½" high, 6⅞" across, $145.00. Sugar with lid, emerald w/gold trim, 7" high, 4¼" across, $95.00. Creamer, emerald w/gold trim, 5⅛" high, 5⅞" across, $95.00.

Not Shown: Butter dish, crystal, $70.00. Spooner, emerald w/gold trim, $75.00.

Pattern: Columbia with Pie Crust Edge
Manufacturer: Dalzell, Gilmore & Leighton, Findlay, Ohio
Date Introduced: c. 1893
Colors Made: Crystal, crystal w/etch
Items/Values: Butter dish, 5⅞" high, 7½" across, $65.00. Creamer, 4½" high, 5⅞" across, $45.00. Spooner, 4¼" high, 3⅞" across, $45.00.
Not Shown: Sugar with lid, $60.00.
Notes: Values for plain crystal pieces are 10% less than crystal w/etch. Values given are for crystal w/etch.

Pattern: Comet in the Stars, OMN: U.S. Glass No. 15150
Manufacturer: U.S. Glass Company, c. 1913; Fenton Art Glass, c. 1960s
Date Introduced: c. 1913
Colors Made: Crystal, crystal w/gold
Items/Values: Berry sugar, open, crystal, 6⅞" across 3½" high, $25.00.
Not Shown: Butter dish, $55.00. Sugar with lid, $40.00. Creamer, $30.00. Spooner, $30.00.

Pattern: Connecticut, OMN: U.S. Glass No. 15068
Manufacturer: U.S. Glass Company, Pittsburgh, Pennsylvania, at factory "K"
Date Introduced: c. 1900
Colors Made: Crystal, crystal w/enamel decorations, crystal w/etch
Items/Values: Creamer, crystal, 4¾" high, 5⁵⁄₁₆" across, $40.00.
Not Shown: Butter dish, $50.00. Sugar with lid, $45.00. Spooner, $35.00.

Pattern: Cord Drapery, AKA: Indiana Tumbler No. 350

Manufacturer: Indiana Tumbler & Goblet Company, c. 1900; National Glass, c. 1901; Indiana Glass Company, c. 1907

Date Introduced: c. 1898

Colors Made: Amber, cobalt, emerald

Items/Values: Butter dish, crystal, 6⅛" high, 7¼" across, $150.00.

Not Shown: Sugar with lid, $95.00. Creamer, $75.00. Spooner, $65.00.

Pattern: Corner Medallion, OMN: No. 720

Manufacturer: Central Glass Company, Wheeling, West Virginia

Date Introduced: c. 1883

Colors Made: Crystal

Items/Values: Butter dish, 7½" high, 7½" across, $170.00. Sugar with lid, 8" high, 4⅞" across, $150.00. Creamer, 4½" high, 6¾" across, $135.00.

Not Shown: Spooner, $100.00.

Pattern: Corrigan
Manufacturer: Dalzell, Gilmore & Leighton, Findlay, Ohio
Date Introduced: c. 1890
Colors Made: Crystal
Items/Values: Butter dish, 5½" high, 7⅜" across, $65.00.
Not Shown: Sugar with lid, $50.00. Creamer, $40.00.
   Spooner, $35.00.

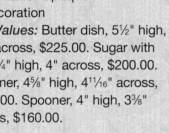

Pattern: Cosmos, AKA: Stemless
   Daisy
Manufacturer: Consolidated Lamp
   and Glass Company
Date Introduced: c. 1902
Colors Made: Opaque
   w/decoration
Items/Values: Butter dish, 5½" high,
   8¼" across, $225.00. Sugar with
   lid, 5¾" high, 4" across, $200.00.
   Creamer, 4⅝" high, 4¹¹⁄₁₆" across,
   $175.00. Spooner, 4" high, 3⅜"
   across, $160.00.

Pattern: Cottage, OMN: Cottage (Adam's, Bellaire No.
   456, goblet only). AKA: Dinner Bell, Fine Cut Band
Manufacturer: Adams & Company, Pittsburgh,
   Pennsylvania, c. 1874; U.S. Glass Company, Pittsburgh,
   Pennsylvania at factory "A" after 1891; Bellaire Goblet
   Company, c. 1891 (goblet only)
Date Introduced: c. 1874
Colors Made: Amber, crystal, crystal w/ruby stain,
   emerald
Items/Values: Butter dish, flat, emerald, 4¾" high, 6⅜"
   across, $175.00.
Not Shown: Sugar with lid, emerald, $150.00. Creamer,
   emerald, $130.00. Spooner, emerald, $125.00.
Notes: Items in amber, blue, crystal w/ruby stain, and
   emerald are considered scarce.

Pattern: Crossed Discs (Disks)
Manufacturer: Unknown
Date Introduced: c. 1890
Colors Made: Crystal
Items/Values: Creamer, 5⅝" high, 4⅞" across, $30.00.
Not Shown: Butter dish, $35.00. Sugar with lid, $30.00.
Spooner, $30.00.

Pattern: Crossed Ovals
Manufacturer: Unknown
Date Introduced: c. 1880s
Colors Made: Crystal
Items/Values: Butter dish, 5½"
high, 8⅛" across, $75.00.
Creamer, 4" high, 5¹¹⁄₁₆" across,
$50.00. Spooner, 3⅜" high, 3¹³⁄₁₆"
across, $45.00. Syrup, 5½" high,
$100.00.
Not Shown: Sugar with lid, $65.00.

Pattern: Crown and Shield, OMN: Persian, Fostoria
No. 576
Manufacturer: Fostoria Glass Company,
Moundsville, West Virginia
Date Introduced: c. 1897
Colors Made: Crystal
Items/Values: Butter dish, 5¼" high, 8" across,
$75.00.
Not Shown: Sugar with lid, $60.00. Creamer, $45.00.
Spooner, $45.00.

Pattern: Cupid and Venus, OMN: Richards & Hartley No. 500. AKA: Guardian Angel, Minerva

Manufacturer: Richards & Hartley Glass Company, Pittsburgh, Pennsylvania, c. 1975; U.S. Glass Company, Pittsburgh, Pennsylvania, 1891

Date Introduced: c. 1875

Colors Made: Crystal

Items/Values: Butter dish, 6¾" high, 6¾" across, $225.00. Milk pitcher, 7⅝" high, 7¾" across, $80.00.

Not Shown: Sugar with lid, $160.00. Creamer, $55.00. Spooner, $45.00.

Pattern: Curtain Tie Back

Manufacturer: Unknown

Date Introduced: c. 1860s

Colors Made: Crystal

Items/Values: Creamer, 5¼" high, 5¾" across, $40.00.

Not Shown: Butter dish, $70.00. Sugar with lid, $50.00. Spooner, $30.00.

Pattern: Cut Log, OMN: Ethol. AKA: Cat's Eye and Block

Manufacturer: Bryce, Higbee & Company, Pittsburgh, Pennsylvania, c. 1889; Westmoreland Specialty Glass Company, Grapeville, Pennsylvania, c. 1896

Date Introduced: c. 1889

Colors Made: Camphor, crystal (other colors rare)

Items/Values: Spooner, crystal, 4⅜" high, 3¾" across, $65.00.

Not Shown: Butter dish, $145.00. Sugar with lid, $115.00. Creamer, $70.00.

Pattern: Dahlia, AKA: Stippled Dahlia
Manufacturer: Portland Glass Company, Portland, Maine; Canton Glass
   Company, Canton, Ohio, c. 1880
Date Introduced: c. 1865
Colors Made: Amber, apple green, crystal, vaseline
Items/Values: Sugar with lid (no lid shown), crystal, 4⅜" across, $70.00.
   Creamer, crystal, 4¹¹⁄₁₆" high, 5" across, $45.00. Spooner, crystal, 4½"
   high, 3⅜" across, $45.00.
Not Shown: Butter dish, crystal, $75.00.

Pattern: Daisy and Button with Narcissus, OMN: Indiana Glass No. 124. AKA: Daisy and
   Button with Clear Lily
Manufacturer: Indiana Glass Company, Dunkirk, Indiana
Date Introduced: c. 1910
Colors Made: Crystal, crystal w/cranberry stain
Reproductions: Flat oval bowls, vases, and wines (amber, dark blue, crystal, green, yellow)
Items/Values: Butter dish, crystal, 5½" high, 7⅜" across, $75.00. Creamer, crystal, 4¼"
   high, 5½" across, $45.00.
Not Shown: Sugar with lid, $65.00. Spooner, $40.00.

Pattern: Daisy Drape
Manufacturer: Unknown
Date Introduced: c. 1870s
Colors Made: Crystal w/stippling
Items/Values: Creamer, 4⅝" high, 5⅛" across, $25.00.
Not Shown: Butter dish, $50.00. Sugar with lid, $40.00.
   Spooner, $25.00.

Pattern: Dakota, AKA: Baby Thumbprint, Thumbprint Band, Thumbprint Band –
   Clear, Thumbprint Band – Red Top
Manufacturer: Ripley & Company, Pittsburgh, Pennsylvania, c. 1885;
   U.S. Glass Company, Pittsburgh, Pennsylvania, c. 1898
Date Introduced: c. 1885
Colors Made: Crystal, crystal w/etch, crystal w/ruby stain
Reproductions: 11" high tankard water pitcher with pressed handle (crystal, crystal
   with light cranberry stain), marked with an embossed "R" within a shield
Items/Values: Butter dish, 6⅛" high, 7½" across, $95.00. Sugar with lid, etching No.
   76 (Fern & Berry), $85.00. Creamer, 6⅜" high, 5½" across, $75.00. Spooner,
   etching No. 76 (Fern & Berry), 6" high, 3¼" across, $60.00.
Notes: Values for plain crystal pieces are 10% less than crystal w/etch. Values given
   are for crystal w/etch pieces.

Pattern: Dalton, AKA: Cradled Diamonds
Manufacturer: Tarentum Glass Company, Tarentum, Pennsylvania
Date Introduced: c. 1904
Colors Made: Crystal, crystal w/gold, crystal w/ruby stain
Items/Values: Butter dish, crystal w/gold $85.00. Milk pitcher, crystal, 7¾" high, 6¼" across, $85.00.
Not Shown: Butter dish, crystal, $75.00. Sugar with lid, crystal, $60.00. Sugar with lid, crystal w/gold, $70.00. Creamer, crystal, $50.00. Creamer, crystal w/gold, $55.00. Spooner, crystal, $50.00. Spooner, crystal w/gold, $55.00. Milk pitcher, crystal w/gold, $95.00.

Pattern: Dalton, AKA: Cradled Diamonds
Manufacturer: Tarentum Glass Company, Tarentum, Pennsylvania
Date Introduced: c. 1904
Colors Made: Crystal, crystal w/gold, crystal w/ruby stain
Items/Values: Celery vase, crystal w/gold, $75.00.
Not Shown: Celery vase, plain crystal, $65.00.

Pattern: Dalzell's Priscilla, OMN: Alexis. AKA: Late Moon and Star, Stelle, Sun and Star
Manufacturer: Dalzell, Gilmore & Leighton, Findlay, Ohio; National Glass Company, Pittsburgh, Pennsylvania, c. 1899
Date Introduced: c. late 1880s
Colors Made: Crystal, crystal w/ruby stain
Reproductions: Many
Items/Values: Butter dish, crystal, 5⅛" high 7½" across, $90.00.
Not Shown: Sugar with lid, $75.00. Creamer, $50.00. Spooner, $45.00.

Pattern: Dart
Manufacturer: Unknown
Date Introduced: c. 1880s
Colors Made: Crystal
Items/Values: Butter dish, 8" high, 6⅛" across, $90.00. Sugar with lid, 9¼" high, 4⅞" across, $95.00. Creamer, 6½" high, 5¾" across, $75.00. Spooner, 6¼" high, 3⅝" across, $75.00.

Pattern: Deer and Pine Tree, OMN: McKee's Band Diamond. AKA: Deer & Doe
Manufacturer: McKee & Brothers, Pittsburgh, Pennsylvania
Date Introduced: c. 1886
Colors Made: Amber, blue, crystal, green (not all items made in color)
Reproductions: Goblet (crystal) by L.G. Wright Glass Company, unmarked
Items/Values: Butter dish, crystal, 5¼" high, 7" across, $300.00. Sugar with lid, crystal, 7⅝" high, 4⅜" across, $200.00. Creamer, crystal, 5⅜" high, 5¾" across, $110.00. Spooner, crystal, 5⅛" high, 3¾" across, $95.00.

Pattern: Delaware, OMN: Diamond's No. 206 – New Century, U.S. Glass No. 15065 – Delaware. AKA: American Beauty, Four Petal Flower
Manufacturer: U.S. Glass Company, Pittsburgh, Pennsylvania
Date Introduced: c. 1899
Colors Made: Crystal, crystal w/rose stain, emerald (plain or w/gold)
Reproductions: 4-pc. table sets
Items/Values: Butter dish, rose w/gold, 4⅜" high, 7¼" across, $175.00. Sugar with lid, rose w/gold, 5¾" high, 3⅞" across, $150.00. Creamer, rose w/gold, 4¾" high, 5¼" across, $95.00. Spooner, rose w/gold, 3¾" high, 3¼" across, $95.00. Celery vase, rose w/gold, 5½" high, 3⅝" across, $115.00.

Pattern: Dewdrop and Raindrop, OMN: Kokomo No. 50, Federal No. 50, AKA: Dew with Raindrop, Dewdrop and Rain
Manufacturer: Kokomo Glass Company, Kokomo, Indiana, c. 1901; Federal Glass Company, Columbus, Ohio c. 1913 – 1914; Indiana Glass Company, Dunkirk, Indiana, c. 1902
Date Introduced: c. 1901
Colors Made: Crystal
Reproductions: Wine in crystal
Items/Values: Butter dish, 5" high, 7⅛" across, $110.00. Sugar with lid, 6⅜" high, 4⅛" across, $85.00. Creamer, crystal, 4½" high, 5" across, $70.00. Spooner, 4⅛" high, 3½" across, $60.00. Jelly compote, 6½" high, 4½" across, $90.00.

Pattern: Dewdrop with Star, AKA: Dewdrop and Star, Dewdrop with Small Star, Star and Dewdrop
Manufacturer: Campbell, Jones & Company, Pittsburgh, Pennsylvania, designed by Jenkins Jones and patented under the design patent Nos. 10096 and 10297, July 17, 1877
Date Introduced: c. 1877
Colors Made: Crystal
Items/Values: Butter dish, 6⅞" high, 7" across, $60.00.
Not Shown: Sugar with lid, $50.00. Creamer, applied handle, $60.00. Creamer, pressed handle, $30.00. Spooner, $30.00.

Pattern: Dewey, OMN: Flower Flange
Manufacturer: Indiana Tumbler & Goblet Company, Dunkirk, Indiana; Indiana Glass Company, c. 1905
Date Introduced: c. 1898
Colors Made: Amber, canary, crystal, emerald
Items/Values: Butter dish, amber, 6⅜" high, 7" across, $140.00. Sugar with lid, amber, 6⅞" high, 5⅛" across, $110.00. Creamer, amber, 4¾" high, 5½" across, $85.00.
Not Shown: Spooner, amber, $70.00.
Notes: Values for crystal pieces are 10% less than amber. Values given are for amber pieces.

Pattern: Diagonal Band with Fan, OMN: Greek
Manufacturer: Ripley & Company, c. 1880s; U.S. Glass Company, c. 1891
Date Introduced: c. 1880s
Colors Made: Crystal
Items/Values: Butter dish, 5⅜" high, 6¼" across, $60.00.
Not Shown: Sugar with lid, $45.00. Creamer, $40.00. Spooner, $35.00.

Pattern: Diamond Block with Fan
Manufacturer: Challinor, Taylor & Company, c. 1885; U.S. Glass Company, c. 1891
Date Introduced: c. 1885
Colors Made: Crystal
Items/Values: Sugar with lid, 9¼" high, 4¼" across, $45.00.
Not Shown: Butter dish, $60.00. Creamer, $30.00. Spooner, $30.00.

Pattern: Diamond Bridges
Manufacturer: U.S. Glass Company, No. 15040
Date Introduced: c. 1895
Colors Made: Crystal, emerald
Items/Values: Sugar with lid, crystal, 6½" high, 3¾" across, $40.00.
Not Shown: Butter dish, $55.00. Creamer, $30.00. Spooner, $30.00.

Pattern: Diamond Flute, AKA: Flamboyant
Manufacturer: McKee & Brothers, Pittsburgh, Pennsylvania, 1864 – 1888; Jeannette, Pennsylvania, 1888 – 1900
Date Introduced: c. 1885
Colors Made: Crystal, emerald (very rare)
Items/Values: Celery vase, crystal, 6¼" high, 4" across, $45.00.
Not Shown: Butter dish, $55.00. Sugar with lid, $40.00. Creamer, $35.00. Spooner, $35.00.

Pattern: Diamond Point Discs, AKA: Diamond Point Disk, Crescent No. 601
Manufacturer: J.B. Higbee Glass Company, c. 1905; New Martinsville Glass Manufacturing Company, 1916
Date Introduced: c. 1905
Colors Made: Crystal
Items/Values: Butter dish, 5½" high, 8" across, $90.00. Sugar with lid, 7¼" high, 4" across, $80.00. Relish/celery tray, 2⅛" high, 5" across, 11⅝" long, $45.00.
Not Shown: Creamer, $70.00. Spooner, $60.00.

Pattern: Diamond Point Loop
Manufacturer: Unknown
Date Introduced: c. 1890s
Colors Made: Amber, blue, canary, crystal (all w/etch)
Items/Values: Butter dish, 6⅝" high, 5" aross, $75.00. Sugar with lid, 7¾" high, 4" across, $60.00. Creamer, 5⅝" high, 5½" across, $60.00. Spooner, 5½" high, 3⁵⁄₁₆" across, $55.00.
Notes: Values for plain crystal pieces are 10% less than amber pieces. Values given are for amber pieces.

Pattern: Diamond Pyramids, AKA: Beaded Triangle, Inverted Imperial
Manufacturer: Indiana Tumbler & Goblet Company; McKee & Brothers, Belmont Glass Company; Federal Glass Company, 1902 – 1914; in sequence at four factories
Date Introduced: c. 1902
Colors Made: Crystal
Items/Values: Spooner, 3¾" high, 3¹³⁄₁₆" across, $30.00.
Not Shown: Butter dish, $65.00. Sugar with lid, $55.00. Creamer, $40.00.

Pattern: Diamond Waffle, OMN: U.S. Glass No. 15025. AKA: U.S. Diamond Block, Patricia
Manufacturer: George Duncan Sons & Company, c. 1880s; U.S. Glass Company, c. 1892
Date Introduced: c. 1880s
Colors Made: Crystal
Items/Values: Butter dish, 5½" high, 7⅜" across, $55.00.
Not Shown: Sugar with lid, $45.00. Creamer, $40.00. Spooner, $40.00.

Pattern: Diamonds with Double Fans
Manufacturer: Indiana Glass Company, Dunkirk, Indiana
Date Introduced: c. 1907
Colors Made: Crystal, crystal w/ruby stain
Items/Values: Spooner, crystal w/ruby stain, 4½" high, 3½" across, $50.00.
Not Shown: Butter dish, crystal w/ruby stain, $100.00. Sugar with lid, crystal w/ruby stain, $85.00. Creamer, crystal w/ruby stain, $65.00.

Pattern: Dolphin, AKA: Dolphin Stem
Manufacturer: Hobbs, Brockunier & Company
Date Introduced: c. 1880s
Colors Made: Crystal, crystal w/frost
Items/Values: Creamer, 6⅞" high, $150.00.
Not Shown: Butter dish, $375.00. Sugar with lid, $325.00.
    Spooner, $140.00.
Notes: Values given are for plain crystal pieces; add 50% for
    crystal w/frost pieces.

Pattern: Double Dahlia with Lens, AKA: Dahlia with/and Petals
Manufacturer: U.S. Glass Company, Pittsburgh, Pennsylvania
Date Introduced: c. 1905
Colors Made: Crystal, crystal w/decoration, emerald, rose blush
    (plain or w/gold trim)
Items/Values: Spooner, rose blush w/gold, 4" high, 3½" across,
    $55.00.
Not Shown: Butter dish, rose blush, $100.00. Sugar with lid,
    rose blush, $90.00. Creamer, rose blush, $70.00.

Pattern: Double Fan
Manufacturer: Dalzell, Gilmore & Leighton, Findlay, Ohio
Date Introduced: c. 1890
Colors Made: Crystal
Items/Values: Celery vase, crystal, 7¹⁄₁₆" high, 4⅜" across, $30.00.
Not Shown: Butter dish, $40.00. Sugar with lid, $35.00. Creamer,
    $35.00. Spooner, $30.00.
Notes: Extended table service includes celery vase.

Pattern: Double Pinwheel, AKA: Juno
Manufacturer: Beatty-Brady Glass Company, c. 1898; Indiana Glass Company, c. 1908
Date Introduced: c. 1898
Colors Made: Crystal
Items/Values: Butter dish, 5⅜" high, 7⅜" across, $45.00.
Not Shown: Sugar with lid, $35.00. Creamer, $30.00. Spooner, $30.00.

Pattern: Duncan's No. 72
Manufacturer: Duncan Glass, was manufactured around 1905, taken from a catalog with no cover. For years former employees have indicated the catalog was issued around 1900.
Date Introduced: c. 1905
Colors Made: Crystal, crystal w/gold decoration
Items/Values: Butter dish, crystal, gold decal around lid, 6½" high, 7½" across, $90.00.
Not Shown: Sugar with lid, $80.00. Creamer, $65.00. Spooner, $50.00.

Pattern: Effulgent Star, OMN: Pattern 876. AKA: Star Galaxy, Star
Manufacturer: Central Glass Company, Wheeling, West Virginia
Date Introduced: c. 1880
Colors Made: Crystal
Items/Values: Jelly compote, 5⁹⁄₁₀" high, 5⅛" across, $75.00.
Not Shown: Butter dish, $95.00. Sugar with lid, $75.00. Creamer, $60.00. Spooner, $40.00.

Pattern: Egg in Sand, AKA: Bean, Stippled Oval
Manufacturer: Unknown
Date Introduced: c. 1880
Colors Made: Crystal
Items/Values: Butter dish, 4" high, 6⅜" across, $75.00. Sugar with lid (no lid shown), 4" across, $75.00. Creamer, 4½" high, 5" across, $50.00. Spooner, 4⅛" high, 3¼" across, $45.00.

Pattern: Egyptian, AKA: Parthenon
Manufacturer: Adams & Company, Pittsburgh, Pennsylvania
Date Introduced: c. 1880
Colors Made: Crystal
Reproductions: 13¼", 8¼", "Salt Lake Temple" bread platter, embossed "(c) 1983 LDS," signifying "Latter Day Saints."
Items/Values: Butter dish, 5¼" high, 6½" across, $300.00. Sugar with lid, 7½" high, 4¼" across, $250.00.
Not Shown: Creamer, $75.00. Spooner, $55.00.

Pattern: Electric, OMN: U.S. Glass No. 15038
Manufacturer: U.S. Glass Company
Date Introduced: c. 1896
Colors Made: Crystal
Items/Values: Butter dish, 6¼" high, 8" across, $75.00. Celery vase, 6⅝"
   high, 3¾" across, $60.00. Jelly compote, open, 5" high, 5¾" across, $45.00.
Not Shown: Sugar with lid, $60.00. Creamer, $55.00. Spooner, $50.00.

Pattern: Elephant Toes, OMN: U.S. Glass No. 15134
Manufacturer: U.S. Glass Company
Date Introduced: c. 1912
Colors Made: Crystal, crystal w/amethyst or green stain
Items/Values: Sugar with lid, 6" high, 4⅞" across, $65.00. Creamer, 4⅜"
   high, 5½" across, $50.00. Spooner, 3⅞" high, 3⅛" across, $50.00.
Not Shown: Butter dish, $80.00.
Notes: Values for plain crystal pieces are 25% less than values for other
   pieces. Values given are for crystal w/stain.

Pattern: Empress, OMN: Riverside No. 492.
  AKA: Double Arch
Manufacturer: Riverside Glass Works,
  Wellsburg, West Virginia
Date Introduced: c. 1898
Colors Made: Crystal, crystal w/gold, emerald
  w/gold
Items/Values: Butter dish, emerald w/gold, 5⅝"
  high, 7½" across, $160.00.
Not Shown: Sugar with lid, emerald, $140.00.
  Creamer, emerald, $110.00. Spooner, emerald,
  $95.00.

Pattern: Empress, OMN: Riverside No.
  492. AKA: Double Arch
Manufacturer: Riverside Glass Works,
  Wellsburg, West Virginia
Date Introduced: c. 1898
Colors Made: Crystal, crystal w/gold,
  emerald w/gold
Items/Values: Butter dish, crystal w/gold,
  5⅝" high, 7½" across, $115.00. Sugar
  with lid, crystal w/gold, 6⅜" high, 4¾"
  across, $100.00. Spooner, crystal w/gold,
  4⅞" high, 3⅝" across, $65.00.
Not Shown: Creamer, crystal w/gold,
  $75.00.

Pattern: Era
Manufacturer: Bryce, Higbee & Company
Date Introduced: c. mid-1880s
Colors Made: Crystal
Items/Values: Butter dish, 6¾" high, 7" across, $85.00.
Not Shown: Creamer, $65.00. Sugar with lid, $70.00.
  Spooner, $45.00.

Pattern: Esther, OMN: Esther Ware. AKA: Tooth and Claw
Manufacturer: Riverside Glass Works, Wellsburg,
West Virginia
Date Introduced: c. 1896
Colors Made: Crystal, crystal w/amber stain, crystal w/ruby stain, emerald (plain or w/gold)
Items/Values: Butter dish, crystal, 5⅝" high, 7¾" across, $90.00.
Not Shown: Sugar with lid, crystal, $80.00. Creamer, crystal, $60.00. Spooner, crystal, $55.00.

Pattern: Esther, OMN: Esther Ware.
AKA: Tooth and Claw
Manufacturer: Riverside Glass Works,
Wellsburg, West Virginia
Date Introduced: c. 1896
Colors Made: Crystal, crystal w/amber stain, crystal w/ruby stain, emerald (plain or w/gold)
Items/Values: Sugar with lid, emerald w/gold, 6½" high, 4⅝" across, $130.00. Spooner, emerald w/gold, 4⅝" high, 3½" across, $90.00.
Not Shown: Butter dish, emerald w/gold, $155.00.

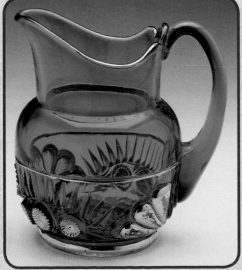

Pattern: Esther, OMN: Esther Ware.
AKA: Tooth and Claw
Manufacturer: Riverside Glass Works, Wellsburg, West Virginia
Date Introduced: c. 1896
Colors Made: Crystal, crystal w/amber stain, crystal w/ruby stain, emerald (plain or w/gold)
Items/Values: Creamer, emerald w/gold, $100.00.

Pattern: Eureka
Manufacturer: National Glass Company at McKee & Brothers, Jeannette, Pennsylvania
Date Introduced: c. 1901 – 1904
Colors Made: Crystal, crystal w/ruby stain
Items/Values: Butter dish, crystal, 5¼" high, 8" across, $80.00. Creamer, crystal, 4⅝" high, 5⅛" across, $45.00. Toothpick holder, crystal, 2½" high, 2¼" across, $40.00.
Not Shown: Sugar with lid, $65.00. Spooner, $60.00.

Pattern: Evangeline, OMN: U.S. Glass No. 15131
Manufacturer: U.S. Glass Company, Gas City, Indiana
Date Introduced: c. 1909
Colors Made: Crystal, crystal w/decoration (plain or w/gold)
Items/Values: Butter dish, crystal w/painted flowers, gold trim, 5⅞" high, 7⅜" across, $65.00. Sugar with lid, crystal w/painted flowers, gold trim, 6¼" high, 7⅞" across, $50.00. Creamer, crystal w/painted flowers, gold trim, 4" high, 5⅝" across, $40.00. Spooner, crystal w/painted flowers, gold trim, 4⅛" high, 6⅝" across, $30.00.

Pattern: Eyewinker, AKA: Cannon Ball, Crystal Ball, Winking Eye

Manufacturer: Attributed to the Dalzell, Gilmore & Leighton Glass Company, Findlay, Ohio

Date Introduced: c. 1889

Colors Made: Crystal

Reproductions: Some in crystal and colors by L.G. Wright Company

Items/Values: Butter dish, 6" high, 7⅜" across, $175.00. Sugar with lid, 6⅜" high, 4" across, $200.00. Milk pitcher, 7¼" high, 7½" across, $350.00.

Not Shown: Creamer, $135.00. Spooner, $120.00.

Pattern: Fagot, OMN: Robinson No. 1. AKA: Vera

Manufacturer: Robinson Glass Company, Zanesville, Ohio

Date Introduced: c. 1893

Colors Made: Crystal, crystal w/frost

Items/Values: Sugar with lid, crystal w/frost, 6⅛" high, 3⅝" across, $65.00.

Not Shown: Butter dish, crystal w/frost, $85.00. Creamer, crystal w/frost, $50.00. Spooner, crystal w/frost, $40.00.

Pattern: Fancy Loop, OMN: 1205, 1205½

Manufacturer: A.H. Heisey & Company

Date Introduced: c. 1896

Colors Made: Crystal, crystal w/gold, emerald, emerald w/gold

Items/Values: Sugar with lid, crystal, 6⅝" high, 3¾" across, $90.00. Creamer, crystal w/gold, 4⅞" high, 5⅛" across, $60.00. Spooner, crystal, 4½" high, 3⅜" across, $60.00. Cruet with stopper (no stopper shown), crystal, 4¾" high, 3¼" across, $75.00.

Not Shown: Butter dish, crystal, $140.00.

Pattern: Fandango, OMN: 1201
Manufacturer: A.H. Heisey & Company
Date Introduced: c. 1896
Colors Made: Crystal, crystal w/gold
Items/Values: Salt shaker, $65.00.
Not Shown: Butter dish, $145.00. Sugar with lid, $90.00.
Creamer, $75.00. Spooner, $70.00.
Notes: Add 10% for pieces w/gold.

Pattern: Fan with Diamond, OMN: McKee
No. 3 – Shell
Manufacturer: McKee & Brothers,
Pittsburgh, Pennsylvania
Date Introduced: c. 1880
Colors Made: Crystal
Items/Values: Butter dish, 4⅛" high, 6⅛"
across, $70.00. Creamer, 5½" high, 4⅞"
across, pressed handle, $45.00. Spooner,
5¼" high, 3½" across, $40.00.
Not Shown: Sugar with lid, $65.00.
Creamer, applied handle, $85.00.

Pattern: Feather, OMN: Cambridge Glass No. 669, McKee's Doric. AKA: Cambridge Feather, Feather and Quill,
Fine Cut and Feather, Indiana Swirl, Prince's Feather, Swirl, Swirl(s) and Feather(s)
Manufacturer: McKee Glass Company, Jeannette, Pennsylvania, c. 1896 –1901; Cambridge Glass Company,
Cambridge, Ohio, c. 1902 – 1903
Date Introduced: c. 1896
Colors Made: Amber stain, crystal, emerald
Reproductions: Goblet (amber, blue, crystal)
Items/Values: Butter dish, crystal, 5¼" high, 7⅛" across, $85.00. Sugar with lid, crystal, 7⅜" high, 4½" across,
$85.00. Creamer, crystal, 4½" high, 5⅛" across, $45.00. Spooner, 4⁹⁄₁₆" high, 3⅜" across, scalloped rim, $45.00.
Not Shown: Spooner, smooth rim, $35.00.

Pattern: Feather Band
Manufacturer: U.S. Glass Company, Pittsburgh, Pennsylvania
Date Introduced: c. 1910
Colors Made: Crystal
Items/Values: Butter dish, 5½" high, 7¼" across, $45.00.
Not Shown: Sugar with lid, $40.00. Creamer, $30.00. Spooner, $25.00.

Pattern: Feather Duster, OMN: U.S. Glass No. 15043. AKA: Huckle, Rosette Medallion
Manufacturer: U.S. Glass Company, Pittsburgh, Pennsylvania
Date Introduced: c. mid-1895
Colors Made: Crystal, emerald
Items/Values: Butter dish, plain rim, crystal, 4⅞" high, 6½" across, $65.00. Sugar with lid (no lid shown), crystal, 4⅜" across, $55.00. Creamer, crystal, 5⅛" high, 5⅜" across, $45.00. Celery vase, crystal, 6¾" high, 3¾" across, $45.00.
Not Shown: Butter dish, crystal, flanged rim, $85.00. Spooner, crystal, $35.00.

Pattern: Ferris Wheel, AKA: Lucile
Manufacturer: Indiana Glass Company, Dunkirk, Indiana
Date Introduced: c. 1910
Colors Made: Crystal, crystal w/gold
Items/Values: Butter dish, crystal w/gold, $65.00. Spooner, crystal, 3¾" high, 3⅞" across, $40.00. Cruet with stopper, crystal, 6¾" high, 3⅜" across, $75.00.
Not Shown: Butter dish, crystal, $60.00. Sugar, open, crystal, 4⅛" high, 6¾" across, $50.00. Sugar with lid, crystal w/gold, $50.00. Creamer, crystal, $40.00. Creamer, crystal, trimmed in gold, 4⅝" high, 5½" across, $45.00. Spooner, crystal w/gold, $45.00. Cruet with stopper, crystal w/gold, $85.00.

Pattern: Festoon
Manufacturer: Beatty-Brady Glass Company, Dunkirk, Indiana
Date Introduced: c. 1898
Colors Made: Crystal
Items/Values: Butter dish, 5¼" high, 6¾" across, $110.00. Creamer, 4½" high, 4¾" across, $50.00.
Not Shown: Sugar with lid, $85.00. Spooner, $35.00.

Pattern: Field Thistle, AKA: Jungle, Flaming Thistle
Manufacturer: U.S. Glass Company
Date Introduced: c. 1912
Colors Made: Crystal, crystal w/ruby stain (plain or w/gold)
Items/Values: Butter dish, crystal w/ruby, gold, 5⅝" high, 7¾" across, $110.00. Sugar with lid (no lid shown), crystal w/ruby, gold, 4⅛" across, $95.00. Creamer, crystal w/ruby, gold, 4⅞"high, 5¹³⁄₁₆" across, $80.00. Spooner, crystal w/ruby, gold, 4⅝" high, 3⅝" across, $80.00.

Pattern: Fine Cut Band
Manufacturer: Unknown
Date Introduced: c. late 1880s or early 1890s
Colors Made: Crystal, crystal w/gold
Items/Values: Butter dish, crystal w/gold, 5⅞" high, 8¼" across, $75.00.
Not Shown: Sugar with lid, crystal w/gold, $60.00. Creamer, crystal w/gold, $50.00. Spooner, crystal w/gold, $40.00.

Pattern: Fish Scale, OMN: Coral
Manufacturer: Bryce Brothers, Pittsburgh, Pennsylvania, c. 1888; U.S. Glass Company, Pittsburgh, Pennsylvania, c. 1891 – 1898
Date Introduced: c. 1888
Colors Made: Crystal, crystal w/ruby stain (scarce)
Items/Values: Butter dish, crystal, 5¼" high, 7⅛" across, $85.00. Sugar with lid, crystal, 7½" high, 4¼" across, $75.00. Creamer, crystal, 5⅛" high, 5⅛" across, $60.00. Spooner, crystal, 4⅞" high, 3⅜" across, $55.00.

Pattern: Fleur-de-Lis and Drape, OMN: U.S. Glass No. 15009.
AKA: Fleur-de-Lis and Tassel
Manufacturer: Adams & Company, c. 1888; U.S. Glass Company,
Pittsburgh, Pennsylvania, factory "A," c. 1891
Date Introduced: c. 1888
Colors Made: Crystal, emerald
Reproductions: Some exist, marked with "D" in heart or "B" in
diamond
Items/Values: Butter dish, crystal, flat, 5" high, 6¼" across, $65.00.
Sugar with lid, crystal, 7⅞" high, 4⅛" across, $65.00. Creamer,
crystal, 5½" high, 5¼" across, $50.00. Spooner, crystal, 5" high,
3½" across, $50.00. Celery vase, crystal, 6¾" high, 3¾" across,
$65.00.
Not Shown: Butter dish, crystal, footed, flanged rim, $80.00.

Pattern: Florida, OMN: U.S. Glass No. 15056
– Florida. AKA: Emerald Green Herringbone
(emerald green only), Paneled Herringbone
(crystal only), Prism and Herringbone
Manufacturer: U.S. Glass Company,
Pittsburgh, Pennsylvania, at factory "B"
Date Introduced: c. 1898
Colors Made: Crystal, emerald
Reproductions: Goblet and square plate
Items/Values: Butter dish, 5⅝" high, 6⅜"
across, $85.00. Jelly compote, open, 4½"
high, 5⅝" across.
Not Shown: Sugar with lid, $80.00. Creamer,
$70.00. Spooner, $70.00.
Notes: Values for crystal pieces are 20% less
than emerald. Values given are for emerald
pieces.

Pattern: Flower and Diamond, OMN: U.S. Glass No. 15147
Manufacturer: U.S. Glass Company
Date Introduced: c. 1913
Colors Made: Crystal, crystal w/gold, crystal w/green stain
Items/Values: Butter dish, crystal w/green stain and gold trim, 4⅝" high, 7⅞" across, $85.00.
Not Shown: Sugar with lid, $70.00. Creamer, $55.00. Spooner, $45.00.

Pattern: Flower and Honeycomb
Manufacturer: U.S. Glass Company
Date Introduced: c. 1915
Colors Made: Crystal, crystal w/green and maroon flowers
Items/Values: Creamer, 5½" high, 5¾" across, $40.00.
Not Shown: Butter dish, $55.00. Sugar with lid, $45.00. Spooner, $35.00.
Notes: Values given are for pieces with crystal w/green and maroon flowers. Values for plain crystal pieces are 15% less.

Pattern: Flower Pot, AKA: Potted Plant, Flower Plant
Manufacturer: Unknown
Date Introduced: c. late 1870s – early 1880s
Colors Made: Crystal w/stippling
Items/Values: Butter dish, 5⁷⁄₁₆" high, 7½" across, $85.00. Sugar with lid (no lid shown), $75.00. Creamer, 4½" high, 5⅝" across, $60.00.
Not Shown: Spooner, $45.00.

Pattern: Flower with Cane, AKA: Diamond Gold
Manufacturer: U.S. Glass Company No. 15141 (Glassport)
Date Introduced: c. 1912
Colors Made: Crystal, crystal w/gold, crystal w/green, crystal w/rose
Items/Values: Sugar with lid, crystal w/rose and gold stain, 6¼" high, 4½" across, $85.00. Creamer, crystal w/rose and gold stain, 4½" high, 5½" across, $75.00. Spooner, crystal w/rose and gold stain, 4¼" high, 4" across, $75.00. Jelly compote, open, crystal w/rose and gold stain, 4⅛" high, 4⅞" across, $80.00.
Not Shown: Butter dish, crystal w/rose and gold stain, $100.00.

Pattern: Fort Pitt, OMN: U.S. Glass No. 15123
Manufacturer: U.S. Glass Company
Date Introduced: c. 1910
Colors Made: Crystal
Items/Values: Butter dish, 6" high, 8¼" across, $40.00.
Not Shown: Sugar with lid, $35.00. Creamer, $30.00. Spooner, $30.00.

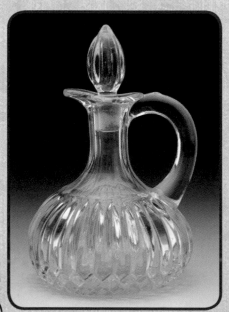

Pattern: Fostoria, OMN: Nickel-Plate No. 27, AKA: Seely
Manufacturer: Nickel Plate Glass Company, c. 1888; U.S. Glass Company, c. 1891
Date Introduced: c. 1888
Colors Made: Crystal
Items/Values: Cruet with original stopper, 6¼" high, $60.00.
Not Shown: Butter dish, $45.00. Sugar with lid, $40.00. Creamer, $35.00. Spooner, $30.00.

Pattern: Fostoria's Atlanta, OMN: Fostoria No. 500 – Atlanta. AKA: Clear Lion Head, Frosted Atlanta, Late Lion, Square Lion, Square Lion Heads

Manufacturer: Fostoria Glass Company, Moundsville, West Virginia

Date Introduced: c. 1895

Colors Made: Crystal, crystal w/frost (plain or w/etch)

Items/Values: Butter dish, crystal, 5¼" high, 6¾" across, $160.00. Sugar with lid, 7⅛" high, 3¼" across, $150.00. Creamer, 5" high, 3⅛" across, $125.00. Spooner, 4½" high, 3¼" across, $100.00. Jelly compote, open, scalloped rim, crystal, 4⅛" high, 4⅜" across, $90.00.

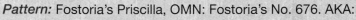

Pattern: Fostoria's Priscilla, OMN: Fostoria's No. 676. AKA: Acanthus Leaf

Manufacturer: Fostoria Glass Company, Moundsville, West Virginia

Date Introduced: c. 1898

Colors Made: Crystal, emerald

Items/Values: Butter dish, crystal, 5¾" high, 8" across, $135.00.

Not Shown: Sugar with lid, $90.00. Creamer, $70.00. Spooner, $55.00.

Pattern: Frisco, OMN: No. 1229

Manufacturer: Fostoria Glass Company, Moundsville, West Virginia

Date Introduced: c. 1904

Colors Made: Crystal

Items/Values: Creamer, 4½" high, 5" across, $40.00.

Not Shown: Butter dish, $60.00. Sugar with lid, $50.00. Spooner, $35.00.

Pattern: Frontier, OMN: New Martinsville No. 718. AKA: Colonial &
   Mitre
Manufacturer: New Martinsville Glass Manufacturing Company
Date Introduced: c. 1911
Colors Made: Crystal, crystal w/gold, crystal w/ruby stain
Items/Values: Butter dish, crystal w/gold, 6¼" high, 8½" across,
   $65.00. Sugar with lid, crystal w/gold, 7⅝" high, 4½" across, $60.00.
   Spooner, crystal w/gold, 4¼" high, 4⅛" across, $45.00.
Not Shown: Creamer, crystal w/gold, $50.00.

Pattern: Frosted Chicken, OMN: No.
   76 Ware. AKA: Chick, Chicken
Manufacturer: Riverside Glass Works,
   Wellsburg, West Virginia
Date Introduced: c. late 1880s
Colors Made: Crystal, crystal w/etch
Items/Values: Butter dish, crystal,
   6¾" high, 6⅞" across handle to
   handle, $250.00. Sugar with lid,
   crystal, 8" high, 6⅜" across,
   $225.00. Celery vase, crystal
   w/etch, 8⅛" high, 6½" across,
   $105.00.
Not Shown: Butter dish, crystal
   w/etch, $275.00. Sugar with lid,
   crystal w/etch, $275.00. Creamer,
   crystal, $85.00. Creamer, crystal
   w/etch, $95.00. Spooner, crystal,
   $75.00. Spooner, crystal w/etch,
   $85.00.

Pattern: Frosted Circle, OMN: U.S. Glass No. 15007 – Horn of Plenty. AKA: Crystal Circle (without frosting)

Manufacturer: Bryce Brothers, Pittsburgh, Pennsylvania, c. 1876; U.S. Glass Company, Pittsburgh, Pennsylvania, after 1891

Date Introduced: c. 1876

Colors Made: Crystal, crystal w/frost

Reproductions: Goblet (crystal), unmarked

Items/Values: Sugar with lid, crystal, 8" high, 4⅛" across, $50.00.

Not Shown: Butter dish, $75.00. Creamer, $40.00. Spooner, $30.00.

Notes: Values for frosted pieces are 15% more than crystal. Values given are for crystal pieces.

Pattern: Frosted Eagle, AKA: Frosted Hawk, Old Abe

Manufacturer: Attributed by early researchers to the Crystal Glass Company, Bridgeport, Ohio

Date Introduced: c. 1883

Colors Made: Crystal, crystal w/frost

Items/Values: Sugar with lid, crystal w/frost, 8⅞" high, 6½" across, $180.00.

Not Shown: Butter dish, handle with double rings, $250.00. Butter dish, no handle, $160.00. Creamer, $80.00. Spooner, $70.00.

Pattern: Frosted Ribbon, OMN: Duncan's No. 150. AKA: Ribbon

Manufacturer: George Duncan & Sons, Pittsburgh, Pennsylvania, c. 1878 - 1886; U.S. Glass Company, Pittsburgh, Pennsylvania, after 1891

Date Introduced: c. 1878 – 1886

Colors Made: Crystal, crystal w/etch, crystal w/frost

Items/Values: Butter dish, 7⅞" high, 6⁷⁄₁₆" across, $65.00. Creamer, 6⁷⁄₁₆" high, 5½" across, $45.00. Spooner, 6⅜" high, 3¾" across, $40.00.

Not Shown: Sugar with lid, $55.00.

Notes: Values for crystal w/frost pieces and crystal w/etch pieces are 20% more than plain crystal pieces. Values given are for plain crystal pieces.

Pattern: Gala, AKA: Hawaiian Lei, Daisy with X Band
Manufacturer: J.B. Higbee Glass Company, 1913;
    Jefferson Glass Company, Toronto, after 1919; Mosser
    Glass Inc., after 1971 (children's table sets only)
Date Introduced: c. 1913
Colors Made: Crystal
Items/Values: Butter dish, 7½" across, 4½" high, $65.00.
Not Shown: Sugar with lid, $45.00. Creamer, $30.00.
    Spooner, $30.00.

Pattern: Galloway, OMN: U.S. Glass No. 15086 – Mirror, Jefferson's No. 15061. AKA: Mirror Plate,
    U.S. Mirror, Virginia, Woodrow
Manufacturer: U.S. Glass Company, Pittsburgh, Pennsylvania, c. 1904; Jefferson Glass
    Company, Toronto, Canada, between 1900 and 1925
Date Introduced: c. 1900
Colors Made: Crystal, crystal w/rose (plain or w/gold)
Items/Values: Butter dish, crystal, 6¾" high, 8⅛" across, $85.00. Sugar with lid, crystal, 7⅜" high,
    4⅞" across, $85.00. Creamer, crystal, 4⅜" high, 5½" across, $55.00. Spooner, crystal, 4⅛"
    high, 4⅛" across, $40.00.

Pattern: Garfield Drape, AKA: Canadian Drape
Manufacturer: Attributed by early researchers to Adams & Company, Pittsburgh, Pennsylvania
Date Introduced: c. 1880s
Colors Made: Crystal
Items/Values: Sugar with lid (no lid shown), 4½" across, $125.00. Creamer, pressed handle, 5½" high, 5¼" across, $65.00. Spooner, 5⅛" high, 3½" across, $50.00.
Not Shown: Butter dish, hard to find, $175.00. Creamer, applied handle, $110.00.

Pattern: Garfield Drape, AKA: Canadian Drape
Manufacturer: Attributed by early researchers to Adams & Company, Pittsburgh, Pennsylvania
Date Introduced: c. 1880s
Colors Made: Crystal
Items/Values: Butter dish (lid only shown), note finial, 3¾" high, 5½" across, $175.00.

Pattern: Gem, AKA: Nailhead
Manufacturer: Bryce, Higbee & Company, Pittsburgh, Pennsylvania
Date Introduced: c. 1885
Colors Made: Crystal, crystal w/aquamarine, crystal w/orange
Items/Values: Butter dish, crystal, 4⅞" high, 7⅛" across, $85.00. Sugar with lid, crystal, 7⅛" high, 4¼" across, $80.00. Creamer, crystal, 5¼" high, 5" across, $65.00. Spooner, crystal, 5" high, 3½" across, $55.00.

Pattern: Geneva, AKA: "Shell and Scroll"
Manufacturer: National Glass Company/McKee
Date Introduced: c. 1900
Colors Made: Crystal, custard, decorated, emerald
Items/Values: Butter dish, plain or w/gold, $125.00.
Not Shown: Sugar with lid, $110.00. Creamer, $95.00.
   Spooner, $80.00.

Pattern: Georgia, OMN: U.S. Glass
   No. 15076 – Georgia. AKA:
   Peacock Eye, Peacock Feather(s)
Manufacturer: Richards & Hartley
   Glass Company, Pittsburgh,
   Pennsylvania; U.S. Glass Company
   at factory "E"
Date Introduced: c. 1902
Colors Made: Crystal
Items/Values: Butter dish, 5¼" high,
   7⅛" across, $95.00. Sugar with
   lid, 6⅜" high, 4⅜" across, $100.00.
   Creamer, 4½" high, 5½" across,
   $80.00. Spooner, 4¼" high, 4"
   across, $90.00.

Pattern: Georgia Gem, OMN: Little Gem
Manufacturer: Tarentum Glass Company
Date Introduced: c. 1900
Colors Made: Crystal, crystal w/gold, custard
Items/Values: Butter dish, crystal w/gold, 5⅝" high,
   7½" across, $90.00.
Not Shown: Sugar with lid, crystal w/gold, $80.00. Creamer,
   crystal w/gold, $65.00. Spooner, crystal w/gold, $50.00.
Notes: Values for crystal pieces are 10% less than crystal
   w/gold. Values given are for crystal w/gold pieces.

Pattern: Gibson Girl, OMN: Medallion
Manufacturer: McKee-Jeannette Glass Company
Date Introduced: c. 1904
Colors Made: Crystal, crystal w/frost
Items/Values: Butter dish, crystal, 5⅝" high, 6⅞"
  across, $350.00.
Not Shown: Sugar with lid, $250.00. Creamer,
  $125.00. Spooner, $110.00.

Pattern: Good Luck, AKA: Horseshoe, Prayer Mat, Prayer Rug
Manufacturer: Adams & Company, Pittsburgh, Pennsylvania
Date Introduced: c. 1891
Colors Made: Crystal, colors rare
Reproductions: Small oval bread platter with single horseshoe
  handle (crystal), unmarked
Items/Values: Sugar with lid, crystal, 7⅜" high, 4¼" across, $135.00.
Not Shown: Butter dish, $150.00. Creamer, $45.00. Spooner, $40.00.

Pattern: Grand, OMN: New Grand. AKA:
  Diamond Medallion, Fine Cut &
  Diamond, Fine Cut Medallion
Manufacturer: Bryce, Higbee &
  Company, Pittsburgh, Pennsylvania
Date Introduced: c. 1885
Colors Made: Crystal, crystal w/ruby stain
Items/Values: Butter dish, crystal, flat, 5"
  high, 6⅜" across, $70.00. Sugar with
  lid, crystal, plain rim, 6¾" high, 4¹/₁₆"
  across, $75.00. Creamer, crystal, 6"
  high, 5⅜" across, $60.00. Spooner,
  crystal, 4½" high, 3¼" across, $50.00.
  Celery vase, crystal, 7¹³/₁₆" high, 4¼"
  across, $95.00.
Not Shown: Butter dish, crystal, footed,
  $90.00. Sugar with lid, crystal, scalloped
  rim, $85.00.

Pattern: Grape and Cable
Manufacturer: Northwood Company, Wheeling, West Virginia
Date Introduced: c. 1900
Colors Made: Carnival, crystal
Items/Values: Butter dish, crystal w/gold trim, 5⅞" high, 7¾" across,
    $175.00. Sugar with lid, crystal w/gold trim, 6⅜" high, 4¾" across,
    $150.00. Creamer, crystal w/gold trim, 4¼" high, 5⅛" across, $125.00.
    Spooner, crystal w/gold trim, 3¹⁵⁄₁₆" high, 4¼" across, $100.00.

Pattern: Grape and Festoon, OMN: Doyle No. 25, Wreath
Manufacturer: Boston & Sandwich Glass Company,
    Sandwich, Massachusetts, c. 1880s; Doyle
    & Company, Pittsburgh, Pennsylvania; U.S. Glass
    Company, Pittsburgh, Pennsylvania, c. 1891
Date Introduced: c. 1880s
Colors Made: Crystal, crystal leaf, stippled grape,
    stippled leaf, veined leaf
Items/Values: Butter dish, crystal, 4" high, 6⅛" across,
    $75.00.
Not Shown: Sugar with lid, $75.00. Creamer, $50.00.
    Spooner, $40.00.

Pattern: Grape with Vine
Manufacturer: Unknown
Date Introduced: c. 1900s
Colors Made: Crystal, crystal w/decoration
Items/Values: Butter dish, crystal, 5⅝" high, 7⅜" across,
    $45.00.
Not Shown: Sugar with lid, $35.00. Creamer, $25.00.
    Spooner, $25.00.

Pattern: Grasshopper, AKA: Locust, Long Spear
Manufacturer: Riverside Glass Works, Wellsburg,
   West Virginia
Date Introduced: c. 1883
Colors Made: Crystal, crystal w/etch, crystal w/insect
Items/Values: Butter dish, crystal w/insect, 6¾" high, 6³⁄₁₆" across,
   $260.00. Sugar with lid, crystal w/insect, 8¼" high, 4" across,
   $200.00. Creamer, crystal, 5½" high, 5¾" across, $50.00. Spooner,
   crystal w/insect, 5¼" high, 3½" across, $140.00. Celery vase,
   crystal w/insect, 6⅝" high, 3⅞" across, $245.00.
Not Shown: Sugar with lid, crystal, $60.00. Creamer, crystal w/insect,
   $150.00. Spooner, crystal, $45.00. Celery vase, crystal, $70.00.

Pattern: Grated Diamond &
   Sunburst, OMN: Duncan
   No. 20
Manufacturer: George
   Duncan & Sons, Pittsburgh,
   Pennsylvania
Date Introduced: c. 1895
Colors Made: Crystal, crystal
   w/gold
Items/Values: Butter dish,
   crystal, 5¼" high, 8" across,
   $85.00. Sugar with lid,
   crystal, 7" high, 3¾" across,
   $70.00. Creamer, crystal,
   4¼" high, 4⅞" across,
   $55.00. Spooner, crystal,
   4⅛" high, 3" across, $55.00.

Pattern: Greensburg's No. 130, AKA: Block Barrel
Manufacturer: Greensburg Glass Company, Greensburg,
  Pennsylvania, 1889 – 1892
Date Introduced: c. 1889
Colors Made: Crystal
Items/Values: Butter dish, 5¼" high, 7⅜" across, $70.00. Creamer,
  4⅝" high, 5½" across, $45.00. Spooner, 4⅜" high, 3⅞" across,
  $45.00. Jam jar with lid, 4⅞" high, 3⅜" across, $75.00.
Not Shown: Sugar with lid, $60.00.

Pattern: Grenade
Manufacturer: Unknown in most books. Ron Teal, Sr. attributes this pattern to Model
  Flint, Albany, Indiana
Date Introduced: Unknown
Colors Made: Crystal, crystal w/gold
Items/Values: Butter dish, 6" high, 7¼" across, $75.00. Sugar w/lid (no lid shown), 3⅞"
  across, $65.00. Spooner, 4½" high, 3⅝" across, $50.00. Celery vase, 6¼" high,
  4⅜" across, $85.00.
Not Shown: Creamer, $55.00.

Pattern: Grille
Manufacturer: Unknown
Date Introduced: Unknown
Colors Made: Crystal
Items/Values: Sugar with lid (no lid shown),
 5¾" across, $60.00.
Not Shown: Butter dish, $75.00. Creamer,
 $50.00. Spooner, $40.00.

Pattern: Hanover, AKA: Block with Stars, Blockhouse,
 Hanover Star
Manufacturer: Richards & Hartley Glass Company,
 Tarentum, Pennsylvania, c. 1888; U.S. Glass Company,
 Pittsburgh, Pennsylvania, after 1891
Date Introduced: c. 1888
Colors Made: Amber, blue, crystal, vaseline
Items/Values: Creamer, crystal, 4¼" high, 5¼" across,
 $35.00.
Not Shown: Butter dish, $50.00. Sugar with lid, $40.00.
 Spooner, $25.00.

Pattern: Hartley, OMN: U.S. Glass No. 900. AKA: Daisy and
 Button with Oval Panels, Paneled Diamond Cut and Fan
Manufacturer: Richards & Hartley Glass Company, Tarentum,
 Pennsylvania, c. 1887; U.S. Glass Company, Pittsburgh,
 Pennsylvania, c. 1891
Date Introduced: c. 1887
Colors Made: Amber, blue, canary, crystal
Items/Values: Celery vase, crystal, 7" high, 4½" across,
 $35.00.
Not Shown: Butter dish, crystal, $50.00. Sugar with lid,
 crystal, $45.00. Creamer, crystal, $30.00. Spooner,
 crystal, $25.00.

Pattern: Harvard Yard, AKA: Tarentum Harvard
Manufacturer: Tarentum Glass Company, Tarentum, Pennsylvania
Date Introduced: c. 1896
Colors Made: Crystal (plain or w/gold), crystal w/ruby stain, emerald, pink
Items/Values: Butter dish, 6¼" high, 8" across, $75.00. Sugar with lid, 7½" high, 4⅝" across, $65.00. Creamer, 4⅝" high, 5¾" across, $45.00. Spooner, 4½" high, 3⅞" across, $40.00.
Notes: Values for plain crystal pieces are 10% less than other pieces. Values given are for crystal w/gold pieces.

Pattern: Heart Stem
Manufacturer: Unknown
Date Introduced: c. 1880s or 1890s
Colors Made: Crystal
Items/Values: Butter dish, 7" high, 7¾" across, $90.00. Creamer, 6⅜" high, 5³⁄₁₆" across, $65.00.
Not Shown: Sugar with lid, $80.00. Spooner, $50.00.

Pattern: Heart with Thumbprint, OMN: Tarentum's Hartford. AKA: Bull's Eye in Heart, Columbia, Columbian, Heart and Thumbprint
Manufacturer: Tarentum Glass Company, Tarentum, Pennsylvania
Date Introduced: c. 1898
Colors Made: Crystal, crystal w/ruby, emerald
Items/Values: Butter dish, crystal, 5⅞" high, 7⅞" across, $240.00.
Not Shown: Sugar with lid, $195.00. Creamer, $135.00. Spooner, $90.00.

Pattern: Heavy Drape, AKA: No. 1300
Manufacturer: Fostoria Glass Company, Moundsville, West Virginia
Date Introduced: c. 1904
Colors Made: Crystal, crystal w/gold
Items/Values: Butter dish, 6¾" high, 7⅞" across, $100.00.
Not Shown: Sugar with lid, $85.00. Creamer, $70.00. Spooner, $60.00.
Notes: Values for plain crystal pieces are 10% less than crystal w/gold. Values given are for crystal w/gold pieces.

Pattern: Heavy Finecut, OMN: Duncan No. 800. AKA: Bagware
Manufacturer: George Duncan & Sons, Pittsburgh, Pennsylvania, c. 1883; U.S. Glass Company, c. 1891
Date Introduced: c. 1883
Colors Made: Amber, blue, crystal, vaseline
Items/Values: Spooner, crystal, 4½" high, 3½" across, $40.00.
Not Shown: Butter dish, $60.00. Sugar with lid, $50.00. Creamer, $45.00.

Pattern: Heavy Gothic, OMN: U.S. Glass No. 15014. AKA: Whitton
Manufacturer: Columbia Glass Company, Findlay, Ohio, c. 1890;
  U.S. Glass Company, Pittsburgh, Pennsylvania, c. 1891
Date Introduced: c. 1890
Colors Made: Crystal, crystal w/ruby stain
Reproductions: Goblet in crystal, amber, and blue by Redcliff USA
Items/Values: Sugar with lid, crystal, 6⅞" high, 4⅜" across, $65.00.
  Creamer, crystal, 4¾" high, 5½" across, $45.00. Celery vase, crystal,
  5¾" high, 4¼" across, $50.00.
Not Shown: Butter dish, crystal, $75.00. Spooner, crystal, $45.00.

Pattern: Heavy Panelled Finecut, OMN: No. 800 Fine Cut Four Panel. AKA: Panelled Diamond Cross
Manufacturer: George Duncan & Sons, c. 1883; U.S. Glass Company, c. 1891
Date Introduced: c. 1883
Colors Made: Amber, blue, crystal, vaseline
Items/Values: Butter dish, crystal, 7¼" high, 5¾" across, $70.00. Sugar with lid, crystal, 8⅝" high,
  4" across, $60.00. Creamer, crystal, 6" high, 5⅝" across, $55.00. Spooner, crystal, 5⅞" high, 3⅛"
  across, $40.00.

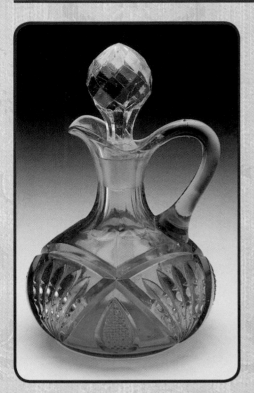

Pattern: Heisey's Pineapple & Fan, OMN: 1255
Manufacturer: Heisey Glass, A.H. Heisey & Company, Newark, Ohio
Date Introduced: c. 1898
Colors Made: Crystal, emerald (plain or w/gold)
Items/Values: Cruet, emerald w/gold, $245.00.
Notes: Values for crystal pieces are 20% less than values for emerald.

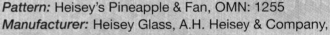

Pattern: Heisey's Pineapple & Fan, OMN: 1255
Manufacturer: Heisey Glass, A.H. Heisey & Company,
   Newark, Ohio
Date Introduced: c. 1898
Colors Made: Crystal, emerald (plain or w/gold)
Items/Values: Butter dish, emerald w/gold, 5⅜" high,
   7½" across, $300.00.
Not Shown: Sugar with lid, emerald w/gold, $250.00.
   Creamer, emerald w/gold, $200.00. Spooner,
   emerald w/gold, $160.00.
Notes: Values for crystal pieces are 20% less than
   values for emerald pieces.

Pattern: Hero, AKA: Ruby Rosette
Manufacturer: Elson Glass Company, Martins Ferry, Ohio, c. 1891; West Virginia Glass
   Company, Martins Ferry, Ohio, c. 1893
Date Introduced: c. 1891
Colors Made: Crystal, enameled decoration, ruby stain
Items/Values: Butter dish, 6⅛" high, 7½" across, $90.00.
Not Shown: Sugar with lid, $85.00. Creamer, $70.00. Spooner, $60.00.
Notes: Values for crystal pieces are 20% less than values for other pieces.

Pattern: Herringbone Band
Manufacturer: Unknown
Date Introduced: Unknown
Colors Made: Crystal
Items/Values: Spooner, 4⅞" high, $45.00.
Not Shown: Butter dish, $80.00. Sugar with lid,
$65.00. Creamer, $45.00.

Pattern: Hexagonal Bull's Eye, AKA: Creased
Hexagon Block, Double Red Block (red stained)
Manufacturer: Dalzell, Gilmore & Leighton,
Findlay, Ohio, 1888 – 1902
Date Introduced: c. 1895
Colors Made: Crystal
Items/Values: Sugar with lid, 6½", $65.00. Creamer,
4⅞" high, 5½" across, $50.00
Not Shown: Butter dish, $90.00. Spooner, $45.00.

Pattern: Hickman, AKA: La Clede, Jubilee No. 1, Empire
Manufacturer: McKee & Brothers, Jeannette, Pennsylvania, 1888 – 1900; Federal Glass, c. 1914
Date Introduced: c. 1897
Colors Made: Crystal, crystal w/amber, crystal w/gold, emerald (plain or w/gold)
Items/Values: Butter dish, crystal w/gold, 4⅞" high, 7¾" across, $75.00. Creamer, crystal, 4¾" high, 5⅜"
across, $45.00. Celery vase, crystal, 6" high, 4¼" across, $65.00.
Not Shown: Butter dish, crystal, $65.00. Sugar with lid, crystal, $50.00. Sugar with lid, crystal w/gold,
$55.00. Creamer, crystal w/gold, $50.00. Spooner, crystal, $45.00. Spooner, crystal w/gold, $50.00.
Celery vase, crystal w/gold, $75.00.

Pattern: Hidalgo, OMN: Adams' No. 5. AKA: Frosted Waffle, Waffle – Red Top

Manufacturer: Adams & Company, Pittsburgh, Pennsylvania, c. 1880; U.S. Glass Company, Pittsburgh, Pennsylvania, c. 1891

Date Introduced: c. 1880

Colors Made: Crystal, crystal w/amber, crystal w/decoration, crystal w/frost, crystal w/ruby

Items/Values: Butter dish, crystal w/frost, 6⅞" high, 5½" across, $70.00. Sugar with lid, crystal w/frost, 8⅜" high, 4⅛" across, $60.00. Creamer, crystal w/frost, 5⅜" high, 6⅛" across, $45.00.

Not Shown: Spooner, crystal w/frost, $45.00.

Pattern: High Hob, OMN: Westmoreland No. 550

Manufacturer: Westmoreland Specialty Glass Company, Grapeville, Pennsylvania

Date Introduced: c. 1915

Colors Made: Crystal, crystal w/ruby

Items/Values: Butter dish, crystal, 4⅜" high, 7⅜" across, $45.00.

Not Shown: Sugar with lid, $40.00. Creamer, $30.00. Spooner, $30.00.

Pattern: Hobbs' Block, OMN: Hobbs' No. 330. AKA: Divided Squares
Manufacturer: Hobbs, Brockunier & Company, Wheeling, West Virginia,
    c. 1888; U.S. Glass Company, Pittsburgh, Pennsylvania, c. 1891
Date Introduced: c. 1888
Colors Made: Crystal, crystal w/amber, crystal frosted w/amber
Reproductions: Some in crystal w/amber, or frost
Items/Values: Butter dish, 4⅝" high, 6³⁄₁₆" across, $110.00. Sugar with
    lid (no lid shown), 5⅝" across, $95.00. Creamer, 4" high, 5¾" across,
    $80.00. Spooner, 3¾" high, 4⅜" across, $75.00.

Pattern: Hobnail Pointed
    (Ball Feet)
Manufacturer: Adams &
    Company, Pittsburgh,
    Pennsylvania, made prior
    to joining U.S. Glass
    Company in 1891
Date Introduced: c. 1891
Colors Made: Crystal
Items/Values: Butter dish,
    4¾" high, 7¼" across,
    $150.00. Sugar with lid, 6⅝"
    high, 4⅞" across, $125.00.
    Creamer, 4¾" high, 4¾"
    across, $95.00. Spooner,
    4½" high, 3¾" across,
    $95.00.

Pattern: Horseshoe Daisy, OMN: No. 717
Manufacturer: New Martinsville Glass Manufacturing Company, New Martinsville, West Virginia
Date Introduced: c. 1912
Colors Made: Crystal, crystal w/gold, crystal w/ruby stain (plain or w/gold)
Items/Values: Butter dish, crystal w/gold, 6⅜" high, 8½" across, $95.00. Sugar with lid, crystal w/gold, 6½" high, 6⅝" across, $80.00. Creamer, crystal w/gold, 4⅛" high, 5½" across, $75.00. Spooner, crystal w/gold, 4" high, $80.00.

Pattern: Illinois, OMN: U.S. Glass No. 15052. AKA: Clarissa, Star of the East
Manufacturer: U.S. Glass Company, Pittsburgh, Pennsylvania, at factory "G" and factory "P"
Date Introduced: c. 1897
Colors Made: Crystal, crystal w/ruby stain, emerald
Reproductions: Covered butter dish (amber, blue, crystal, pink), celery vase (crystal white opalescent), unmarked
Items/Values: Butter dish, crystal, 5½" high, 7" across, $90.00. Creamer, crystal, 2⅞" high, 6" across, $65.00.
Not Shown: Sugar with lid, $95.00. Spooner, $35.00.

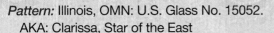

Pattern: Indiana, OMN: U.S. Glass No. 15029. AKA: Prison Window(s)
Manufacturer: U.S. Glass Company, factory "U," Gas City, Indiana
Date Introduced: c. 1897
Colors Made: Crystal, crystal w/gold, crystal w/ruby stain (plain or w/gold)
Items/Values: Butter dish, 5¼" high, 7¼" across, $105.00. Sugar with lid (no lid shown), 4¼" across, $95.00. Creamer, 3⅞" high, 5⅝" across, $75.00. Spooner, 3⅝" high, 3¼" across, $90.00.
Notes: Values for plain crystal pieces are 10% less than other pieces. Values given are for crystal w/gold pieces.

Pattern: Indiana Feather
Manufacturer: Beatty-Brady Glass Company, Dunkirk, Indiana, c. 1900 to at least 1904
Date Introduced: c. 1900
Colors Made: Crystal
Items/Values: Butter dish, 4⅞" high, 7⅜" across, $80.00. Spooner, 4¼" high, 4¼" across, smooth rim, $35.00.
Not Shown: Sugar with lid, $70.00. Creamer, $45.00. Spooner, scalloped rim, $45.00.

OUR SENSATION ASSORTMENT

Pattern: Indiana Sensation, AKA: "Indiana Silver"
Manufacturer: Indiana Glass Company
Date Introduced: c. 1913
Colors Made: Crystal, crystal w/silver
Items/Values: Butter dish, $65.00. Sugar with lid, $60.00. Creamer, $50.00. Spooner, $45.00.

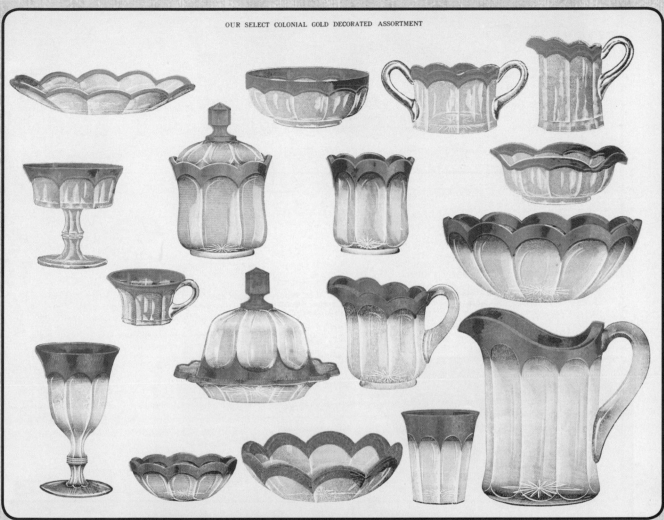

OUR SELECT COLONIAL GOLD DECORATED ASSORTMENT

Pattern: Indiana's Colonial
Manufacturer: Indiana Glass Company
Date Introduced: c. 1913
Colors Made: Crystal (plain or w/gold)
Items/Values: Butter dish, $55.00. Sugar with lid, $40.00.
   Creamer, $35.00. Spooner, $35.00.
Notes: Values for plain crystal pieces are 10% less than
   crystal w/gold. Values given are for crystal w/gold pieces.

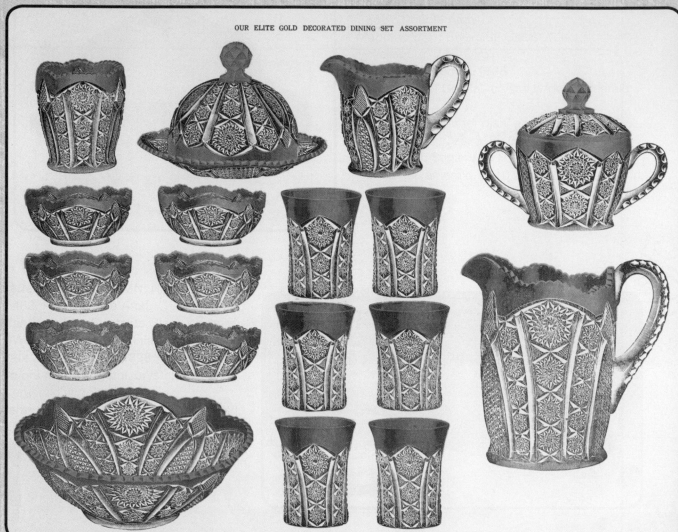

OUR ELITE GOLD DECORATED DINING SET ASSORTMENT

Pattern: Indiana's Elite No. 123, AKA: Panelled Daisy and Fine Cut

Manufacturer: Indiana Glass Company

Date Introduced: c. 1910

Colors Made: Crystal (plain or w/gold)

Reproductions: Many

Items/Values: Butter dish, $70.00. Sugar with lid, $50.00. Creamer, $35.00. Spooner, $35.00.

Notes: Values for plain crystal pieces are 10% less than crystal w/gold. Values given are for crystal w/gold pieces.

OUR TRIUMPH GOLD DECORATED ASSORTMENT

Pattern: Indiana's No. 156, AKA: Horsemint

Pattern: Indiana's No. 156, AKA: Horsemint
Manufacturer: Indiana Glass Company, Dunkirk, Indiana
Date Introduced: c. 1913
Colors Made: Crystal, crystal w/gold
Items/Values: Butter dish, 5⅜" high, 7⅝" across, $60.00.
Not Shown: Sugar with lid, $45.00. Creamer, $35.00.
  Spooner, $35.00.
Notes: Values for crystal w/gold pieces are 10% more
  than crystal. Values given are for crystal pieces.

Pattern: Intaglio, AKA: Flower Spray with Scrolls
Manufacturer: Northwood Glass Company, Indiana, Pennsylvania
Date Introduced: c. 1898
Colors Made: Custard, emerald (plain or w/gold)
Items/Values: Butter dish, custard w/gold and blue trim, 6½" high, 7⅝" across, $280.00. Sugar with lid (no lid shown), custard w/gold and blue, 4¾" across, $185.00.
Not Shown: Creamer, $150.00. Spooner, $125.00.

Pattern: Intaglio Sunflower, OMN: U.S. Glass No. 15125
Manufacturer: U.S. Glass Company at factory "GP" at Glassport, Pennsylvania (factory "O")
Date Introduced: c. 1911
Colors Made: Crystal, crystal w/decoration
Items/Values: Butter dish, crystal, 6" high, 7½" across, $55.00.
Not Shown: Sugar with lid, $40.00. Creamer, $30.00. Spooner, $25.00.

Pattern: Intaglio Sunflower, OMN: U.S. Glass No. 15125
Manufacturer: U.S. Glass Company at factory "GP" at Glassport, Pennsylvania (factory "O")
Date Introduced: c. 1911
Colors Made: Crystal, crystal w/decoration
Item/Value: Celery vase, $35.00.

Pattern: Interlocked Hearts, AKA: Wishbone
Manufacturer: Unknown
Date Introduced: c. 1900
Colors Made: Crystal
Items/Values: Butter dish, 5⅞" high, 7¾"
 across, $50.00.
Not Shown: Sugar with lid, $45.00. Creamer,
 $30.00. Spooner, $25.00.

Pattern: Inverted Strawberry, OMN: Cambridge No.
 2870 – Strawberry. AKA: Late Strawberry Variant
Manufacturer: Cambridge Glass Company
Date Introduced: c. 1915
Colors Made: Crystal, emerald green, ruby stain
Reproductions: Unmarked cruet, plate, toothpick
 holder, tumbler, and water pitcher by Guernsey
 Glass Company, Cambridge, Ohio
Items/Values: Butter dish, crystal, 5⅛" high, 7¼"
 across, $140.00.
Not Shown: Sugar with lid, $100.00. Creamer, $70.00.
 Spooner, $80.00.

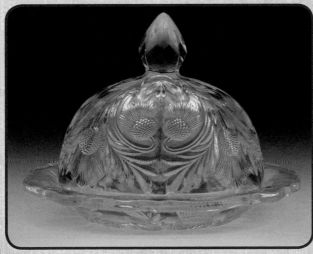

Pattern: Inverted Thistle, AKA: Late Thistle
Manufacturer: Cambridge Glass Company,
 Cambridge, Ohio
Date Introduced: c. 1906
Colors Made: Crystal
Reproductions: Some in colors by Imperial Glass
 Company, c. 1960s
Items/Values: Butter dish, 5⅜" high, 7⁷⁄₁₆"
 across, $60.00.
Not Shown: Sugar with lid, $45.00. Creamer, $30.00.
 Spooner, $30.00.

Pattern: Iowa, OMN: U.S. Glass No. 15069.
  AKA: Panelled Zipper
Manufacturer: U.S. Glass Company
Date Introduced: c. 1900
Colors Made: Crystal, crystal w/gold, crystal
  w/rose blush
Items/Values: Creamer, 3⅛" high, 4" across,
  $50.00.
Not Shown: Butter dish, $85.00. Sugar with lid,
  $70.00. Spooner, $45.00.
Notes: Values given are for crystal w/gold
  pieces. Values for plain crystal are 10% less
  than values for crystal w/gold pieces. Add
  35% for crystal w/rose blush pieces.

Pattern: Iris, AKA: Pineapple, Paden City No. 206
Manufacturer: J.B. Higbee Glass Company, 1917;
  Paden City, 1918; Dalzell-Viking, 1996 (relish tray only).
  Iris design was patented by Samuel Irvine on March 7,
  1916 (patent No. 48688) and assigned to the
  J.B. Higbee Glass Company shortly thereafter.
Date Introduced: c. 1917
Colors Made: Crystal
Items/Values: Butter dish, 5" high, 8¼" across, $50.00.
Not Shown: Sugar with lid, $40.00. Creamer, $30.00.
  Spooner, $30.00.

Pattern: Iris with Meander, AKA: Fleur-de-Lis Scrolled
Manufacturer: Jefferson Glass Company
Date Introduced: c. 1903
Colors Made: Amethyst, blue, crystal, opalescent
  colors (all plain or w/gold)
Items/Values: Butter dish, blue, 6" high, 7⅞" across,
  $300.00.
Not Shown: Sugar with lid, blue, $175.00. Creamer,
  blue, $100.00. Spooner, blue, $100.00.

Pattern: Ivanhoe
Manufacturer: Dalzell, Gilmore & Leighton, Brilliant, Ohio
 – Wellsburg, West Virginia, 1888
Date Introduced: c. 1890
Colors Made: Crystal
Items/Values: Butter dish, 5¼" high, 8" across, $80.00.
Not Shown: Sugar with lid, $65.00. Creamer, $50.00.
 Spooner, $40.00.

Pattern: Ivy in Snow, OMN: Forest. AKA: Forest Ware,
 Ivy in Snow – Red Leaves (ruby stained)
Manufacturer: Co-Operative Flint Glass Company,
 Beaver Falls, Pennsylvania
Date Introduced: c. 1898
Colors Made: Crystal, crystal w/ruby stain, crystal
 w/stippling
Reproductions: Extensive in crystal and white by
 Kemple Glass Works
Items/Values: Butter dish, crystal, w/stippling, 4⅝" high,
 6" across, $75.00. Celery vase, crystal, 7⅞" high, 4⅛"
 across, $65.00.
Not Shown: Sugar with lid, $65.00. Creamer, squat,
 $45.00. Creamer, table-sized tankard, $50.00.
 Spooner, $40.00.

Pattern: Japanese, AKA: Bird in Ring, Butterfly and
 Fan, Grace, Japanese Fan
Manufacturer: George Duncan & Sons, Pittsburgh,
 Pennsylvania
Date Introduced: c. 1880
Colors Made: Crystal
Items/Values: Butter dish (no lid shown), 7" across
 (low standard), footed, $245.00.
Not Shown: Butter dish, flat, $165.00. Sugar with
 lid, $155.00. Creamer, $60.00. Spooner, $55.00.

Pattern: Japanese Iris, OMN: No. 716 – "Rebecca"

Manufacturer: New Martinsville Glass Manufacturing Company, New Martinsville, West Virginia

Date Introduced: c. 1910

Colors Made: Crystal, crystal w/gold, crystal w/ruby stain

Items/Values: Butter dish, 5" high, 8¹⁄₁₆" across, $90.00. Sugar with lid, 5¾" high, 4¼" across, $85.00.

Not Shown: Creamer, $70.00. Spooner, $65.00.

Notes: Values for plain crystal pieces are 10% less than crystal w/gold. Values given are for crystal w/gold pieces.

Pattern: Jasper, AKA: Belt Buckle, Late Buckle

Manufacturer: Bryce Brothers, Pittsburgh, Pennsylvania, c. 1880; U.S. Glass Company, Pittsburgh, Pennsylvania, at factory "B" after 1891

Date Introduced: c. 1880

Colors Made: Crystal, rare in colors

Reproductions: Cake stand, 9" across

Items/Values: Butter dish, crystal, 5½" high, 6¾" across, $80.00. Sugar with lid, crystal, 8½" high, 5¼" across, $70.00.

Not Shown: Creamer, $45.00. Spooner, $35.00.

Pattern: Jeweled Moon & Stars, OMN: Imperial. AKA: Late Moon and Star, Moon and Star Variant, Moon and Star Variation, Moon and Star with Waffle Stem
Manufacturer: Co-Operative Flint Glass Company, Beaver Falls, Pennsylvania
Date Introduced: c. 1896
Colors Made: Crystal, crystal w/color stain, crystal w/frost
Reproductions: Some in crystal, caramel, emerald, white, and pearl luster by Kemple Glass, Phoenix Glass, L.E. Smith, Fenton, and Weishar Enterprises
Items/Values: Celery vase, crystal, $6\frac{5}{8}$" high, $3\frac{15}{16}$" across, $50.00.
Not Shown: Butter dish, $65.00. Sugar with lid, $60.00. Creamer, $40.00. Spooner, $35.00.

Pattern: Jumbo
Manufacturer: Brilliant Glass Works, Brilliant, Ohio
Date Introduced: c. 1881
Colors Made: Crystal, crystal w/frost
Items/Values: Butter dish, crystal, $7\frac{1}{2}$" high, $7\frac{3}{4}$" across, $675.00.
Not Shown: Sugar with lid, $575.00. Creamer, $185.00. Spooner, $180.00.

Pattern: Kansas, OMN: U.S. Glass No. 15072 – Kansas, Kokomo No. 8.
  AKA: Jewel & Dewdrop, Jewel with Dewdrop, Jewel with Dewdrops
Manufacturer: U.S. Glass Company, Pittsburgh, Pennsylvania, c. 1901;
  Kokomo Glass Manufacturing Company, Kokomo, Indiana, c. 1903;
  Federal Glass Company, Columbus, Ohio, c. 1914
Date Introduced: c. 1901
Colors Made: Crystal, crystal w/gold, crystal w/rose stain
Reproductions: Small mug, D.C. Jenkins Glass Company, Kokomo,
  Indiana, unmarked
Items/Values: Butter dish, crystal, 5⅞" high, 6½" across, $165.00. Creamer,
  crystal, 4¾" high, 5⁷⁄₁₆" across, $95.00. Milk pitcher, 1 qt., crystal, 7⅜"
  high, 7½" across, $245.00.
Not Shown: Sugar with lid, $140.00. Spooner, $90.00.

Pattern: Kentucky, OMN: U.S.
  Glass No. 15051 – Kentucky
Manufacturer: U.S. Glass
  Company, Pittsburgh,
  Pennsylvania
Date Introduced: c. 1897
Colors Made: Crystal, crystal
  w/amber or ruby, emerald
  stain
Items/Values: Butter dish,
  crystal, 5⅝" high, 7¾"
  across, $110.00. Cruet with
  original stopper (no stopper
  shown), crystal, $95.00. Celery
  vase, crystal, 7" high, 3⅝"
  across, $60.00.
Not Shown: Sugar with lid,
  $95.00. Creamer, $75.00.
  Spooner, $60.00.

Pattern: King's Crown, OMN: XLCR, Excelsior. AKA: Blue Thumbprint, Ruby Thumbprint, Ruby Thumbprint – Clear

Manufacturer: Adams & Company, Pittsburgh, Pennsylvania c. 1890; U.S. Glass Company, Pittsburgh, Pennsylvania at factory "A," c. 1891

Date Introduced: c. 1890

Colors Made: Crystal, crystal w/rose blush, crystal w/ruby stain (plain or w/gold)

Reproductions: Many, from various companies

Items/Values: Butter dish, crystal w/ruby stain, 5¾" high, 7½" across, $260.00.

Not Shown: Sugar with lid, crystal w/ruby stain, $250.00. Creamer, crystal w/ruby stain, $140.00. Spooner, crystal w/ruby stain, $95.00.

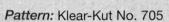

Pattern: Klear-Kut No. 705

Manufacturer: New Martinsville Glass Manufacturing Company, New Martinsville, West Virginia

Date Introduced: c. 1906

Colors Made: Crystal, crystal w/gold, crystal w/ruby stain

Items/Values: Butter dish, crystal, 5¾" high, 8½" across, $85.00.

Not Shown: Sugar with lid, $75.00. Creamer, $60.00. Spooner, $50.00.

Notes: Values for plain crystal pieces are 10% less than other pieces. Values for ruby stain are 25% more. Values given are for crystal w/gold pieces.

Pattern: Klondike, OMN: Dalzell No. 75 & No. 75D, Amberette. AKA: English Hobnail Cross, Frosted Amberette, Klondyke

Manufacturer: Dalzell, Gilmore & Leighton, Findlay, Ohio

Date Introduced: c. 1898

Colors Made: Crystal, crystal w/amber, crystal frosted w/amber

Items/Values: Butter dish, crystal frost w/amber, 5⅞" high, 7" across, $400.00. Sugar with lid, crystal frost w/amber, 6¼" high, 4" across, $325.00. Spooner, crystal frost w/amber, 3½" high, 3½" across, $250.00.

Not Shown: Creamer, crystal frost w/amber, $275.00.

Pattern: Knobby Bull's Eye, OMN: U.S. Glass No. 15155. AKA: Cromwell
Manufacturer: U.S. Glass Company, Glassport, Pennsylvania, factory "GP"
Date Introduced: c. 1915
Colors Made: Crystal, crystal w/amethyst stain, crystal w/green stain/gold (plain or w/gold trim)
Items/Values: Butter dish, crystal w/gold/rose, 5" high, 8¼" across, $90.00.
Not Shown: Sugar with lid, $80.00. Creamer, $60.00. Spooner, $50.00.

Pattern: Knobby Bull's Eye, OMN: U.S. Glass No. 15155. AKA: Cromwell
Manufacturer: U.S. Glass Company, Glassport, Pennsylvania, factory "GP"
Date Introduced: c. 1915
Colors Made: Crystal, crystal w/amethyst stain, crystal w/green stain (plain or w/gold trim), gold
Items/Values: Butter dish, crystal w/gold/green stain, 5" high, 8¼" across, $80.00.
Not Shown: Sugar with lid, $70.00. Creamer, $60.00. Spooner, $45.00.

Pattern: La Belle Rose
Manufacturer: Lancaster Glass Company
Date Introduced: c. 1910
Colors Made: Crystal, goofus
Items/Values: Butter dish, crystal, 5¾" high, 7⅜" across, $60.00.
Not Shown: Sugar with lid, $45.00. Creamer, $30.00. Spooner, $30.00.
Notes: Primarily a Goofus pattern from 1910, this is a sister pattern to Carnation design, Lancaster Glass Company.

Pattern: Lacy Daisy, OMN: U.S. Glass No. 9525. AKA: Daisy
Manufacturer: U.S. Glass Company
Date Introduced: c. 1918
Colors Made: Crystal
Items/Values: Butter dish, 3¾" high, 7¼" across, $95.00. Sugar with lid, 4⅞" high, 4½" across, $65.00. Creamer, 3⅝" high, 5¼" across, $50.00. Spooner, 3¾" high, 3¾" across, $50.00.

Pattern: Ladders, OMN: No. 292 Pattern. AKA: Loop and Pyramid(s)
Manufacturer: Tarentum Glass Company, Tarentum, Pennsylvania
Date Introduced: c. 1901
Colors Made: Crystal, crystal w/gold
Items/Values: Celery vase, crystal, 5⅜" high, 3⅜" across, $35.00. Milk pitcher, crystal, 5¾" high, 6⅛" across, $90.00.
Not Shown: Butter dish, $55.00. Sugar with lid, $45.00. Creamer, $30.00. Spooner, $30.00.

Pattern: Ladders with Diamonds,
OMN: Duncan and Miller No. 52.
AKA: Fine Cut and Ribbed Bars
Manufacturer: Duncan and Miller
Glass Company
Date Introduced: c. 1904
Colors Made: Crystal, crystal w/
gold, crystal w/ruby stain
Items/Values: Sugar with lid,
$50.00. Cruet with original
stopper (no stopper shown),
$95.00. Celery vase, crystal, 5⅜"
high, 3⅝" across, $65.00.
Not Shown: Butter dish, $65.00.
Creamer, $45.00. Spooner,
$45.00.

Pattern: Lattice, AKA: Diamond Bar
Manufacturer: King, Son and Company, c. 1880; U.S.
Glass Company, at factory "K," c. 1891
Date Introduced: c. 1880
Colors Made: Crystal
Items/Values: Butter dish, hexagon knob, lid only
shown, $75.00.
Not Shown: Sugar with lid, $65.00. Creamer, $50.00.
Spooner, $50.00.

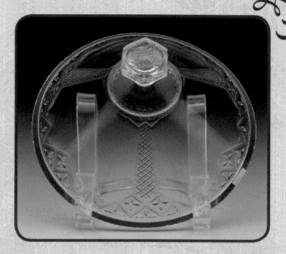

Pattern: Leaf and Flower, OMN: Hobbs'
No. 339
Manufacturer: Hobbs, Brockunier &
Company, Wheeling, West Virginia,
c. 1890; U.S. Glass Company,
Pittsburgh, Pennsylvania, c. 1891
Date Introduced: c. 1890
Colors Made: Crystal w/amber, crystal w/
amber and frost, crystal w/frost
Items/Values: Butter dish, crystal
w/amber, 4⅝" high, 8" across, $125.00.
Not Shown: Sugar with lid, crystal w/amber,
$100.00. Creamer, crystal w/amber,
$85.00. Spooner, crystal w/amber, $70.00.

Pattern: Leaf and Star, OMN: New Martinsville No. 711. AKA: Tobin
Manufacturer: New Martinsville Glass Manufacturing Company, New Martinsville, West Virginia
Date Introduced: c. 1909
Colors Made: Crystal, crystal w/gold, crystal w/ruby stain
Items/Values: Butter dish, 6⅛" high, 8½" across, $75.00. Sugar with lid, 6⅞" high, 4¼" across, $65.00. Creamer, 4¼" high, 5¾" across, $45.00. Spooner, 4⅜" high, 3½" across, $35.00.
Notes: Values for plain crystal pieces are 10% less than other colors. Values listed are for crystal w/gold pieces.

Pattern: Liberty Bell, AKA: Gillinder's Centennial
Manufacturer: Adams & Company, Pittsburgh, Pennsylvania
Date Introduced: c. 1875
Colors Made: Crystal
Reproductions: Goblets and platters
Items/Values: Butter dish, 7½" across, 4½" high, $140.00.
Not Shown: Sugar with lid, $125.00. Creamer, $130.00. Spooner, $65.00.

Liberty Bell, a different view.

Pattern: Lily of the Valley, OMN: Mayflower. AKA: Lily of the Valley on Legs
Manufacturer: Richards & Hartley Flint Glass Company, Tarentum, Pennsylvania
Date Introduced: c. 1870s
Colors Made: Crystal
Items/Values: Spooner, 5⁷⁄₁₆" high, 3⅜" across, pedestal, $70.00.
Not Shown: Butter dish, flat, $135.00. Butter dish, 3-leg, $245.00. Sugar with lid, pedestal, $160.00. Sugar with lid, 3-leg, $185.00. Creamer, 3-leg, $135.00. Creamer, pedestal, $100.00. Spooner, 3-leg, $120.00.

Pattern: Lion and Cable, OMN: Richards & Hartley No. 525 – Proud Lion. AKA: Tiny Lion
Manufacturer: Richards & Hartley Glass Company, Tarentum, Pennsylvania
Date Introduced: c. 1880s
Colors Made: Crystal, crystal w/etch, crystal w/frost
Reproductions: 10½" dia. round tab-handled bread plate, unmarked
Items/Values: Butter dish, crystal w/frost, 7¼" high, 7½" across handle to handle, $140.00. Spooner, double handled, crystal, 6" high, 5½" across, $80.00.
Not Shown: Sugar with lid, $135.00. Creamer, $65.00.

Pattern: Lion, AKA: Frosted Lion
Manufacturer: Gillinder & Sons, Philadelphia, Pennsylvania
Date Introduced: c. 1877
Colors Made: Crystal, crystal w/frost
Reproductions: Tableware by L.G. Wright and Summit Art Glass
Items/Values: Sugar with lid, crystal w/frost, $160.00.
Not Shown: Butter dish, $185.00. Creamer, $90.00. Spooner, $85.00.

Pattern: Long Leaf Teasel, OMN: No. 702
Manufacturer: New Martinsville Glass
   Manufacturing Company
Date Introduced: c. 1906
Colors Made: Crystal
Items/Values: Butter dish, 6" high, 8" across,
   $60.00.
Not Shown: Sugar with lid, $50.00. Creamer,
   $40.00. Spooner, $40.00.

Pattern: Loop and Jewel, AKA: Jewel and Festoon,
   Queen's Necklace, Venus
Manufacturer: National Glass, c. 1903; Indiana
   Glass Company, c. 1906
Date Introduced: c. 1903
Colors Made: Crystal
Items/Values: Butter dish, 5⅞" high, 7¼" across,
   $65.00.
Not Shown: Sugar with lid, $50.00. Creamer, $35.00.
   Spooner, $35.00.

Pattern: Loop with Dewdrop, OMN: U.S. Glass No. 15028
Manufacturer: U.S. Glass Company
Date Introduced: c. 1892
Colors Made: Crystal
Items/Values: Creamer, 4⅞" high, 5¼" across, $40.00.
Not Shown: Butter dish, tab handles, $70.00. Butter dish, no
   handles, $60.00. Sugar with lid, $55.00. Spooner, $35.00.

Pattern: Lorne
Manufacturer: Bryce Brothers, c. 1880s; U.S.
   Glass Company, c. 1891
Date Introduced: c. 1880s
Colors Made: Crystal, vaseline
Items/Values: Butter dish, 3⅞" high, 7½" long, 5"
   across, $85.00.
Notes: This pattern is shown in a company ad
   with a group of butter dishes that were not part
   of a table setting, so we assume there are no
   matching pieces. Lorne is the company name.

Pattern: Louis XV, AKA: Winged Scrolls
Manufacturer: Northwood Glass Company, Indiana,
   Pennsylvania
Date Introduced: c. 1898
Colors Made: Custard w/gold
Items/Values: Butter dish, lid only shown, $220.00.
Not Shown: Sugar with lid, $190.00. Creamer,
   $150.00. Spooner, $135.00.

Pattern: Louise, OMN: Fostoria No. 1121. AKA: Starred Jewel, Sunk Jewel
Manufacturer: Fostoria Glass Company, Moundsville, West Virginia
Date Introduced: c. 1901
Colors Made: Crystal
Items/Values: Butter dish, lid only shown, $75.00. Sugar with lid, 7" high, 4" across, $60.00.
Not Shown: Creamer, $50.00. Spooner, $45.00.

Pattern: Louisiana, OMN: U.S. Glass No. 15053 – Louisiana. AKA: Granby, Sharp Oval and Diamond
Manufacturer: Bryce Brothers, Pittsburgh, Pennsylvania, c. 1870s; reissued by the U.S. Glass Company, Pittsburgh, Pennsylvania, at factory "B," c. 1898
Date Introduced: c. 1870s
Colors Made: Crystal
Items/Values: Butter dish, flanged base, 5¼" high, 7" across, $130.00. Sugar with lid, 7¼" high, 4½" across, $110.00. Creamer, 4¾" high, 5½" across, $75.00. Spooner, 4½" high, 3⅞" across, $90.00.

Pattern: Madeira, OMN: Tarentum No. 300
Manufacturer: Tarentum Glass Company, Tarentum, Pennsylvania
Date Introduced: c. 1912
Colors Made: Crystal, crystal w/ruby stain
Items/Values: Butter dish, crystal, 5¾" high, 7⅞" across, $90.00. Sugar with lid, crystal, 6½" high, 7¼" across, $80.00. Creamer, crystal, 4" high, 5½" across, $65.00. Spooner, crystal, 3⅞" high, 6½" across, $65.00. Celery vase, crystal, 5¾" high, 8" across handle to handle, $90.00.

Pattern: Maine, OMN: U.S. Glass No. 15066. AKA: Paneled Flower, Paneled Stippled Flower, Stippled Paneled Flower, Stippled Primrose
Manufacturer: U.S. Glass Company, Pittsburgh, Pennsylvania
Date Introduced: c. 1899
Colors Made: Crystal, crystal w/enameled decorations, emerald
Items/Values: Milk pitcher, crystal w/stippling, 7⅜" high, 6¾" across, $90.00.
Not Shown: Butter dish, $140.00. Sugar with lid, $135.00. Creamer, $90.00. Spooner, $80.00.
Notes: Values for emerald pieces are 15% higher than plain crystal pieces. Values given are for plain crystal pieces.

Pattern: Manhattan, OMN: U.S. Glass No. 15078 – New York
Manufacturer: U.S. Glass Company, Pittsburgh, Pennsylvania, at factory "G" and factory "P"
Date Introduced: c. 1902
Colors Made: Crystal, crystal w/gold, crystal w/rose stain
Reproductions: Punch set, several other pieces
Items/Values: Creamer, crystal w/gold, table size, trimmed in gold, 3" high, 3¼" across, $50.00. Celery vase, crystal w/gold, $70.00.
Not Shown: Butter dish, crystal, $85.00. Butter dish, crystal w/gold, $95.00. Sugar with lid, table, crystal, $65.00. Sugar with lid, individual, crystal, $30.00. Sugar with lid, table, crystal w/gold, $75.00. Sugar, individual, crystal w/gold, $40.00. Creamer, individual, crystal, $25.00. Creamer, individual, crystal w/gold, $30.00. Creamer, table, crystal w/gold, $60.00. Spooner, crystal, $45.00. Spooner, crystal w/gold, $50.00. Celery vase, crystal, $60.00.

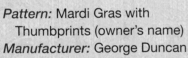

Pattern: Mardi Gras with Thumbprints (owner's name)
Manufacturer: George Duncan and Sons
Date Introduced: Unknown
Colors Made: Crystal, crystal w/amber stain, crystal w/ruby stain, dark amber, sapphire blue
Reproductions: Two vases, punch sets (bowl and cups)
Items/Values: Sugar with lid, crystal, 6½" high, 4¼" across, $85.00. Creamer, crystal, 4½" high, 4⅞" across, $90.00.
Not Shown: Butter dish, $130.00. Spooner, $50.00. Cruet with original stopper, $100.00. Celery vase, $65.00.

Pattern: Mardi Gras, OMN: Duncan No. 42, Empire, AKA: Paneled English Hobnail with Prisms, Siamese Necklace

Manufacturer: Duncan & Miller Glass Company, c. 1898; George Duncan's Sons & Company, Washington, Pennsylvania, c. 1899

Date Introduced: c. 1898

Colors Made: Crystal, crystal w/ruby (plain or w/gold)

Reproductions: Several

Items/Values: Butter dish, crystal, $130.00. Sugar with lid, crystal, 6⅝" high, 4" across, $85.00. Creamer, crystal, 4¼" high, 5½" across, $90.00. Spooner, crystal, 4¼" high, 3¼" across, $50.00. Cruet with original stopper, crystal, 6⅝" high, $100.00. Celery vase, crystal, 5¾" high, 3⅝" across, $65.00.

Pattern: Marlboro, OMN: U.S. Glass No. 15105. AKA: Heart Plume
Manufacturer: U.S. Glass Company, Pittsburgh, Pennsylvania, factory "B"
Date Introduced: c. 1907
Colors Made: Crystal, crystal w/rose (plain or w/gold)
Items/Values: Butter dish, crystal, 4¾" high, 7¼" across, $95.00. Sugar with lid, crystal, 6⅜" high, 7¾" across, $80.00. Creamer, crystal, 3¼" high, 6¼" across, $65.00. Spooner, crystal, 3¼" high, 4⅛" across, $45.00.

Pattern: Marsh Fern, OMN: 327 Pattern
Manufacturer: Riverside Glass Works, Wellsburg, West Virginia
Date Introduced: c. 1889
Colors Made: Crystal, crystal w/etch
Items/Values: Butter dish, crystal, 4⅞" high, 6¾" across, $100.00. Sugar with lid, crystal w/etch, 6¾" high, 3¾" across, $90.00. Creamer, crystal w/etch, 5⅝" high, 4⅜" across, $80.00. Spooner, crystal w/etch, 4½" high, 3⅜" across, $65.00.
Not Shown: Butter dish, crystal w/etch, $110.00. Sugar with lid, crystal, $80.00. Creamer, crystal, $70.00. Spooner, crystal, $55.00.

Pattern: Maryland, OMN: U.S. Glass No. 15049. AKA: Inverted Loop(s) and Fan(s), Loop and Diamond, Loop(s) and Fan(s)

Manufacturer: Bryce Brothers, Pittsburgh, Pennsylvania; U.S. Glass Company, Pittsburgh, Pennsylvania at factory "B"

Date Introduced: c. 1897

Colors Made: Crystal, crystal w/ruby stain

Items/Values: Butter dish, crystal, flat, 4¾" high, 7½" across, $85.00. Butter dish, footed (originally called sweetmeat), 7⅜" high, 7½" across, $110.00. Sugar with lid, crystal, 6¼" high, 4⅛" across, $80.00. Creamer, crystal, 4⅝" high, 5¼" across, $60.00. Spooner, crystal, 4¼" high, 3½" across, $70.00.

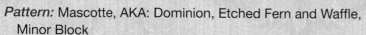

Pattern: Mascotte, AKA: Dominion, Etched Fern and Waffle, Minor Block

Manufacturer: Ripley & Company, Pittsburgh, Pennsylvania; U.S. Glass Company, Pittsburgh, Pennsylvania, at factory "F," c. 1891

Date Introduced: c. 1884

Colors Made: Crystal, crystal w/etch

Reproductions: Jars

Items/Values: Butter dish, 5¾" high, 7¾" across, $100.00

Not Shown: Sugar with lid, $75.00. Creamer, $50.00. Spooner, $40.00.

Pattern: Masonic, AKA: Inverted Prism

Manufacturer: McKee Glass Company, Jeannette, Pennsylvania

Date Introduced: c. 1894

Colors Made: Crystal, emerald (rare)

Items/Values: Butter dish, crystal, 5½" high, 7½" across, $65.00.

Not Shown: Sugar with lid, $50.00. Creamer, $40.00. Spooner, $40.00.

Pattern: Massachusetts, OMN: U.S. Glass No. 15054 – Massachusetts. AKA: Arched Diamond Points, Cane Variant, Geneva, Star and Diamonds

Manufacturer: U.S. Glass Company, Pittsburgh, Pennsylvania, at factory "K"

Date Introduced: c. 1898

Colors Made: Crystal, crystal w/gold

Reproductions: Butter dish in colors and crystal, unmarked

Items/Values: Butter dish, 5¼" high, 8½" across, $90.00. Sugar with lid, 6¼" high, 6¾" across, $80.00. Celery vase, 5¹⁵⁄₁₆" high, 4⅛" across, $85.00.

Not Shown: Creamer, $70.00. Spooner, $65.00.

Pattern: McKee's Comet

Manufacturer: McKee & Brothers, Pittsburgh, Pennsylvania

Date Introduced: c. 1887

Colors Made: Crystal

Items/Values: Butter dish, 9⅞" high, 6¼" across, $110.00. Sugar with lid, 3⅝" across, $125.00. Creamer, 7⅜" high, 4½" across, $90.00. Spooner, 7⅜" high, 2¾" across, $90.00.

Notes: This pattern's pieces are weighty/bulky, and not likely to survive intact.

Pattern: McKee's Gothic, AKA: Spearpoint Band

Manufacturer: McKee-Jeannette Glass Company, Jeannette, Pennsylvania

Date Introduced: c. 1902

Colors Made: Crystal, crystal w/gold, crystal w/ruby stain (plain or w/gold)

Items/Values: Butter dish, 4½" high, 7⅞" across, $80.00. Sugar with lid, 6" high, 4" across, $70.00. Creamer, 4¼" high, 5" across, $65.00. Spooner, 4" high, 3⅝" across, $65.00.

Notes: Values for crystal pieces are 10% less than other pieces. Values given are for crystal w/gold pieces.

Pattern: McKee's Stars & Stripes
Manufacturer: McKee & Brothers, Jeannette, Pennsylvania
Date Introduced: c. 1898
Colors Made: Crystal
Items/Values: Spooner, 4½" high, 3⅞" across, $40.00.
Not Shown: Butter dish, $60.00. Sugar with lid, $50.00. Creamer, $45.00.

Pattern: Medallion, AKA: Hearts and Spades, Spades
Manufacturer: Unknown
Date Introduced: c. 1885
Colors Made: Amber, apple green, blue, canary, crystal
Reproductions: Butter dish, Imperial Glass Corporation, Bellaire, Ohio, marked with entwined "I.G."
Items/Values: Creamer, crystal, 5½" high, 5½" across, $35.00.
Not Shown: Butter dish, $50.00. Sugar with lid, $40.00. Spooner, $25.00.

Pattern: Melrose, AKA: Diamond Beaded Band
Manufacturer: Greensburg Glass Company, Greensburg, Pennsylvania, c. 1889; Brilliant Glass Works, Brilliant, Ohio, c. 1887 – 1888; McKee Brothers, Jeannette, Pennsylvania, c. 1901 (chocolate items); John B. Higbee Glass Company, Bridgeville, Pennsylvania, c. 1907; New Martinsville Glass Manufacturing Company, New Martinsville, West Virginia, c. 1916; Dugan Glass Company (Diamond Glassware Company), Indiana, Pennsylvania, c. 1915
Date Introduced: c. 1889
Colors Made: Crystal
Items/Values: Butter dish, 5¼" high, 7" across, $50.00.
Not Shown: Sugar with lid, $45.00. Creamer, $35.00. Spooner, $30.00.

Pattern: Michigan, OMN: U.S. Glass No. 15077
– Michigan. AKA: Loop & Pillar, Loop with Pillar,
Panelled Jewel
Manufacturer: U.S. Glass Company, Pittsburgh,
Pennsylvania, at factory "G"
Date Introduced: c. 1902
Colors Made: Crystal, crystal w/blue, crystal w/enamel
decorations, crystal w/rose, crystal w/yellow
Reproductions: Some, marked, in various colors
Items/Values: Butter dish, 5¾" high, 8" across,
$95.00.
Not Shown: Sugar with lid, $85.00. Creamer, $70.00.
Spooner, $55.00.

Pattern: Mikado, AKA: Flower and Bud, Blooms and Blossoms
Manufacturer: Northwood & Company, Wheeling, West Virginia
Date Introduced: c. 1906
Colors Made: Crystal, crystal w/decoration
Items/Values: Butter dish, crystal w/red, blue, and yellow
decoration, lid only shown, $250.00.
Not Shown: Sugar, $195.00. Creamer, $150.00. Spooner,
$130.00.

Pattern: Minerva, AKA: Roman
Medallion
Manufacturer: The Boston &
Sandwich Glass Company,
Sandwich, Massachusetts
Date Introduced: c. 1870s
Colors Made: Crystal
Items/Values: Butter dish, 5" high,
6¼" across, $120.00. Sugar with
lid, 6¾" high, 4½" across,
$135.00. Creamer, 5⅜" high,
5¼" across, $70.00. Spooner,
4⅞" high, 3⅝" across, $70.00.
Notes: Table set was made in two
styles.

Pattern: Minnesota, OMN: U.S. Glass No. 15055 – Minnesota. AKA: Mochness (Unitt)

Manufacturer: U.S. Glass Company, Pittsburgh, Pennsylvania, at factory "F" (Ripley & Company) and factory "G" (Gillinder & Sons), Greensburg, Pennsylvania

Date Introduced: c. 1898

Colors Made: Crystal, crystal w/emerald, crystal w/gold, crystal w/ruby stain

Items/Values: Butter dish, crystal, 4½" high, 8½" across, $90.00. Sugar bowl with lid, 5¼" high, 4⅝" across, $80.00. Toothpick holder, three-handled, scalloped rim, $25.00.

Not Shown: Creamer, $65.00. Spooner, $75.00.

Notes: Values for plain crystal are 10% less than crystal w/gold pieces. Values given are for crystal w/gold.

Pattern: Moon and Star, OMN: Palace. AKA: Bull's Eye and Star, Star and Punty

Manufacturer: Adams & Company, Pittsburgh, Pennsylvania; Co-Operative Flint Glass Company, Beaver Falls, Pennsylvania, c. 1896; U.S. Glass Company, Pittsburgh, Pennsylvania, 1890 – 1898

Date Introduced: c. 1888

Colors Made: Crystal, crystal w/frost, crystal w/ruby

Reproductions: Many, in colors and crystal by L.E. Smith Company, Weishar Enterprises, and L. G. Wright Glass Company

Items/Values: Butter dish, crystal, 5⅞" high, 6⅛" across, $90.00. Celery vase, crystal, 6⅝" high, 4¼" across, $70.00.

Not Shown: Sugar with lid, $110.00. Creamer, crystal, 6⅜" high, 5¾" across, $95.00. Spooner, $75.00.

Pattern: Nail, OMN: U.S. Glass No. 15002. AKA: Recessd Pillar – Red Top, Recessed Pillar – Thumbprint Band

Manufacturer: Ripley & Company, Pittsburgh, Pennsylvania, c. 1880s; U.S. Glass Company, Pittsburgh, Pennsylvania, c. 1891

Date Introduced: c. 1880s

Colors Made: Crystal, crystal w/etch, crystal w/ruby

Items/Values: Butter dish, crystal w/etch, 6" high, 7⅞" across, $85.00. Creamer, crystal w/etch, 4¼" high, 5" across, $60.00. Syrup pitcher with lid, crystal, 6⅜" high, 4" across, $110.00.

Not Shown: Butter dish, crystal, $95.00. Sugar with lid, crystal w/etch, $75.00. Sugar with lid, crystal, $85.00. Creamer, crystal, $70.00. Spooner, crystal w/etch, $50.00. Spooner, crystal, w/o etch, $55.00. Syrup, crystal w/etch, $95.00.

Pattern: Nevada, OMN: U.S. Glass No. 15075

Manufacturer: U.S. Glass Company

Date Introduced: c. 1902

Colors Made: Crystal w/enamel, crystal w/transfer decoration

Items/Values: Butter dish, crystal w/transfer, 6¾" high, 6⅝" across, $125.00. Sugar with lid, crystal w/transfer, 7" high, 4⅞" across, $110.00. Creamer, crystal w/transfer, 4⅛" high, 6¼" across, $95.00. Spooner, crystal w/transfer, 4⅛" high, 4¼" across, $85.00.

Pattern: New Era, AKA: Yoke and Circle
Manufacturer: J.B. Higbee Glass Company
Date Introduced: c. 1912
Colors Made: Crystal
Items/Values: Celery tray, 9½" rectangular, $25.00.
Not Shown: Butter dish, $65.00. Sugar with lid, $40.00.
   Creamer, $30.00. Spooner, $30.00.

Pattern: New Hampshire, OMN: U.S. Glass No. 15084
   – New Hampshire. AKA: Bent Buckle, Maiden's Blush,
   Modiste, Red Loop & Fine Cut
Manufacturer: U.S. Glass Company, Pittsburgh,
Pennsylvania
Date Introduced: c. 1903
Colors Made: Crystal, crystal w/gold, crystal w/rose stain
Items/Values: Butter dish, 5½" high, 8¼" across, $125.00.
   Sugar with lid, 6¾" high, 4" across, $110.00. Creamer,
   5" high, 5¼" across, $75.00. Spooner, 4⅜" high, 3⅜"
   across, $65.00.
Notes: Values for plain crystal pieces are 10% less than
   crystal w/gold. Values given are for crystal w/gold pieces.

Pattern: New Jersey, OMN: U.S. Glass No. 15070 – New Jersey. AKA: Loops and Drops, Red Loop &
   Finecut (Millard)
Manufacturer: U.S. Glass Company, Pittsburgh, Pennsylvania, at factory "G" (Gillinder & Sons, Greensburg,
   Pennsylvania), "P" (Doyle & Company, Pittsburgh, Pennsylvania), and "D" (George Duncan & Sons,
   Pittsburgh, Pennsylvania)
Date Introduced: c. 1900 – 1908
Colors Made: Crystal, crystal w/ruby stain (plain or w/gold)
Items/Values: Butter dish, crystal w/gold, 5½" high, 8" across, $95.00. Sugar with lid, crystal w/gold, 6½"
   high, 5" across, $85.00. Creamer, crystal w/gold, 4¼" high, 5⅜" across, $65.00. Spooner, crystal w/gold, 4"
   high, 3½" across, $55.00.
Notes: Values for plain crystal pieces are 10% less than crystal w/gold. Values given are for crystal
   w/gold pieces.

Pattern: No. 75 – Square
Manufacturer: Adams & Company, Pittsburgh, Pennsylvania, c. 1882 – 1887
Date Introduced: c. 1882
Colors Made: Crystal, crystal w/etch
Items/Values: Butter dish, 6⅛" high, 5¼" across, $120.00. Sugar with lid, 7⅝" high, 3¾" across, $95.00.
Not Shown: Creamer, $75.00. Spooner, $60.00.
Notes: Values for plain crystal pieces are 15% less than crystal w/etch. Values given are for crystal w/etch pieces.

Pattern: No. 119, AKA: Starry Night
Manufacturer: Indiana Glass Company, Dunkirk, Indiana
Date Introduced: c. 1909
Colors Made: Crystal
Items/Values: Butter dish, 5¼" high, 7⅜" across, $60.00.
Not Shown: Sugar with lid, $50.00. Creamer, $40.00. Spooner, $35.00.

Pattern: Nogi, AKA: Pendant, Amulet
Manufacturer: Indiana Glass Company – production extended for several years
Date Introduced: c. 1906
Colors Made: Crystal
Items/Values: Butter dish, 5¼" high, 7¼" across, $60.00. Spooner, 3½" high, 3½" across, $25.00.
Not Shown: Sugar with lid, $45.00. Creamer, $30.00.

Pattern: Northwood Hobstar, OMN: No. 12 Line. AKA: Near Cut, Locket
Manufacturer: Northwood & Company, Wheeling, West Virginia
Date Introduced: c. 1904
Colors Made: Crystal, crystal w/ruby stain (plain or w/gold), emerald
Items/Values: Butter dish, crystal w/ruby and gold trim, 5⅝" high, 8"
   across, $150.00. Sugar with lid (no lid shown), crystal w/ruby and
   gold trim, 7⅞" across, $125.00. Creamer, crystal w/ruby and gold
   trim, 3½" high, 6⅝" across, $100.00.
Not Shown: Spooner, $100.00.
Notes: Any item with ruby stain is rare.

Pattern: O'Hara Diamond, OMN: O'Hara's Diamond, U.S. Glass No. 15001. AKA: Star,
   Sawtooth and Star
Manufacturer: O'Hara Glass Company, Pittsburgh, Pennsylvania, c. 1885;
   U.S. Glass Company, Pittsburgh, Pennsylvania, at factory "L," c. 1891
Date Introduced: c. 1885
Colors Made: Crystal, crystal w/ruby stain
Items/Values: Butter dish, crystal w/ruby stain, 5⅜" high, 7¼" across, $165.00. Sugar
   with lid (no lid shown), crystal w/ruby stain, 3⅞" across, $135.00. Creamer, crystal
   w/ruby stain, 5¼" high, 5" across, $90.00.
Not Shown: Spooner, crystal w/ruby stain, $95.00.

Pattern: Ohio, OMN: U.S. Glass No. 15050
Manufacturer: U.S. Glass Company, Pittsburgh, Pennsylvania, factory "F"
Date Introduced: c. 1897
Colors Made: Crystal, crystal w/etch, crystal w/ruby (rare)
Items/Values: Creamer, crystal w/etch, 5¼" high, 5" across, $80.00. Spooner, crystal w/etch, 4⅝" high, 3¼" across, $75.00.
Not Shown: Butter dish, crystal w/etch, $125.00. Sugar with lid, crystal w/etch, $100.00.

Pattern: Ohio Star
Manufacturer: Millersburg Glass Company
Date Introduced: c. 1909
Colors Made: Carnival colors, crystal
Items/Values: Butter dish, crystal, 5¾" high, 8¼" across, $250.00. Sugar with lid, 5¼" high, 7½" across, $200.00. Creamer, crystal, 3⅜" high, 5⅞" across, $150.00. Spooner, crystal, 3⅝" high, 6¼" across, $150.00. Jelly compote, crystal, 4⅝" high, 5¼" across, $125.00.
Notes: This pattern is best known in carnival glass, but a wide assortment of shapes were made in crystal.

Pattern: One-o-One, AKA: Beaded
101, One Hundred and One, 1-0-1
Manufacturer: George Duncan and
Sons, Pittsburgh, Pennsylvania
Date Introduced: c. 1885
Colors Made: Crystal
Reproductions: Goblet (crystal,
colors), unmarked
Items/Values: Sugar with lid,
6⅝" high, 4¹¹⁄₁₆" across, $145.00.
Creamer, 4⅝" high, 4⅞" across,
$65.00. Spooner, 4½" high, 3⅝"
across, $75.00.
Not Shown: Butter dish, $175.00.

Pattern: Oneata, AKA: Chimo
Manufacturer: Riverside Glass Works, Wellsburg,
West Virginia
Date Introduced: c. 1907
Colors Made: Crystal, crystal w/gold, crystal w/rose
blush (plain or w/gold)
Items/Values: Butter dish, crystal w/rose blush and
gold, 4¾" high, 7¼" across, $125.00.
Not Shown: Sugar with lid, crystal w/rose blush,
$100.00. Creamer, crystal w/rose blush, $85.00.
Spooner, crystal w/rose blush, $70.00.

Pattern: Open Rose, AKA: Moss Rose
Manufacturer: Unknown
Date Introduced: c. 1870
Colors Made: Crystal
Reproductions: Goblet, spooner (amber, blue, crystal,
green), Mosser Glass Company, Cambridge, Ohio,
unmarked
Items/Values: Spooner, 5⅝" high, 2⅞" across, $40.00.
Not Shown: Butter dish, $70.00. Sugar with lid, $70.00.
Creamer, $65.00.

Pattern: Oregon, OMN: U.S. Glass No. 15073 – Oregon. AKA: Beaded
  Loop(s), Beaded Ovals
Manufacturer: U.S. Glass Company, Pittsburgh, Pennsylvania
Date Introduced: c. 1901
Colors Made: Crystal
Reproductions: Butter and sugar by Imperial
Items/Values: Butter dish, flanged rim, 5¼" high, 7¼" across, $95.00.
  Sugar with lid, 6¾" high, 4¾" across, $90.00. Creamer, 4¼" high, 5½"
  across, $90.00. Spooner, 4" high, 4" across, $90.00.

Pattern: Orinda, OMN: Ohio Flint No. 92
Manufacturer: Ohio Flint Glass Company under
  National Glass Company. National called this plant
  Lancaster Glass Works.
Date Introduced: c. 1901
Colors Made: Crystal
Items/Values: Sugar with lid, 6¼" high, $50.00.
Not Shown: Butter dish, $65.00. Creamer, $35.00.
  Spooner, $35.00.

Pattern: Ornate Star, AKA: Ladders and Diamonds with Star, Tarentum Star
Manufacturer: Tarentum Glass Company, Tarentum, Pennsylvania
Date Introduced: c. 1907
Colors Made: Crystal, crystal w/ruby stain
Items/Values: Butter dish, lid only shown, star atop lid knob, crystal, $60.00.
Not Shown: Sugar with lid, crystal, $50.00. Creamer, crystal, $35.00. Spooner, crystal, $35.00.

Pattern: Paddlewheel
Manufacturer: Westmoreland Specialty Glass Company
Date Introduced: c. 1905
Colors Made: Crystal, crystal w/gold
Items/Values: Butter dish, crystal, 4⅞" high, 7⅜" across, $50.00. Creamer, crystal, 3⅜" high, 5¾" across, $35.00. Cruet with stopper (not original stopper), crystal w/gold trim, 4³⁄₁₆" high, $85.00.
Not Shown: Butter dish, crystal w/gold trim, $55.00. sugar with lid, crystal, $45.00. Sugar with lid, crystal w/gold, $50.00. Creamer, crystal w/gold, $40.00. Spooner, crystal, $35.00. Spooner, crystal w/gold, $40.00. Cruet, with original stopper, crystal, $75.00.

Pattern: Panama, OMN: U.S. Glass No. 15088. AKA: Fine Cut Bar, Viking
Manufacturer: U.S. Glass Company
Date Introduced: c. 1904
Colors Made: Crystal
Items/Values: Butter dish, lid only shown, $40.00.
Not Shown: Sugar with lid, $35.00. Creamer, $30.00. Spooner, $30.00.

Pattern: Panel Rib and Shell, OMN: Pattern 730
Manufacturer: Central Glass Company, Wheeling, West Virginia
Date Introduced: c. 1880
Colors Made: Crystal
Items/Values: Creamer, 5½" high, 5⅞" across, $80.00.
Not Shown: Butter dish, $125.00. Sugar with lid, $100.00. Spooner, $60.00.

Pattern: Paneled Daisy, OMN: Brazil. AKA: Daisy and Panel
Manufacturer: Bryce Brothers, Pittsburgh, Pennsylvania; U.S. Glass Company, Pittsburgh, Pennsylvania, at factory "B," c. 1891
Date Introduced: c. 1888
Colors Made: Crystal, crystal w/amber, ruby stain
Items/Values: Butter dish, crystal, lid only shown, $55.00 (flat), $85.00 (footed w/flange rim).
Not Shown: Sugar with lid, $60.00. Creamer, $40.00. Spooner, $35.00.

Pattern: Paneled Palm, AKA: Brilliant
Manufacturer: U.S. Glass Company, No. 15095
Date Introduced: c. 1906
Colors Made: Crystal, crystal w/ruby stain
Items/Values: Butter dish, crystal, 4¾" high, 7⅛" across, $40.00.
Not Shown: Sugar with lid, $35.00. Creamer, $20.00. Spooner, $20.00.

Pattern: Paneled Thistle, OMN: Delta. AKA: Canadian Thistle
Manufacturer: J.B. Higbee Glass Company, Bridgeville, Pennsylvania, c. 1910; Jefferson Glass Company, Toronto, Ontario, Canada
Date Introduced: c. 1908
Colors Made: Crystal, crystal w/gold, crystal w/ruby stain
Reproductions: Several
Items/Values: Sugar with lid, 6⅝" high, 6¾" across (handle to handle), $125.00. Creamer, 4⅝" high, 5½" across, $85.00. Spooner, 4³⁄₁₆" high, 6¼" across, $110.00.
Notes: Values for plain crystal pieces are 10% less than others. Values given are for crystal w/gold pieces.

Pattern: Panelled Daisy and Button, OMN: Ellrose. AKA: Daisy & Button Panelled, Single Scallop, Daisy and Button – Single Panel, Paneled Daisy
Manufacturer: George Duncan & Sons, Pittsburgh, Pennsylvania, introduced in March 1885, reissued by U.S. Glass Company, Pittsburgh, Pennsylvania, c. 1892
Date Introduced: c. 1885
Colors Made: Crystal
Items/Values: Celery vase, 6¾" high, 4⅛" across, $35.00.
Not Shown: Butter dish, $50.00. Sugar with lid, $35.00. Creamer, $35.00. Spooner, $30.00.

Pattern: Panelled English Hobnail, AKA: Notched Finecut
Manufacturer: Tarentum Glass Company, Tarentum, Pennsylvania, late 1901 for 1902 market
Date Introduced: c. 1901
Colors Made: Crystal, crystal w/gold, crystal w/ruby stain
Items/Values: Butter dish, crystal w/gold, 5⅛" high, 7⅝" across, $75.00. Sugar with lid (no lid shown), crystal w/gold, 4" across, $60.00. Creamer, crystal w/gold, 4⅜" high, 5" across, $40.00.
Not Shown: Spooner, crystal w/gold, $40.00.

OUR GRAPE RUBY AND GOLD DECORATED DINING SET ASSORTMENT

Pattern: Panelled Grape

Manufacturer: Indiana Glass Company

Date Introduced: c. 1913

Colors Made: Crystal, crystal w/gold, crystal w/ruby decoration and gold

Items/Values: Butter dish, $95.00. Sugar with lid, $80.00. Creamer, $75.00. Spooner, $60.00.

Notes: Values for plain crystal pieces are 20% less than crystal w/ruby decoration and gold. Values given are for crystal w/ruby decoration and gold.

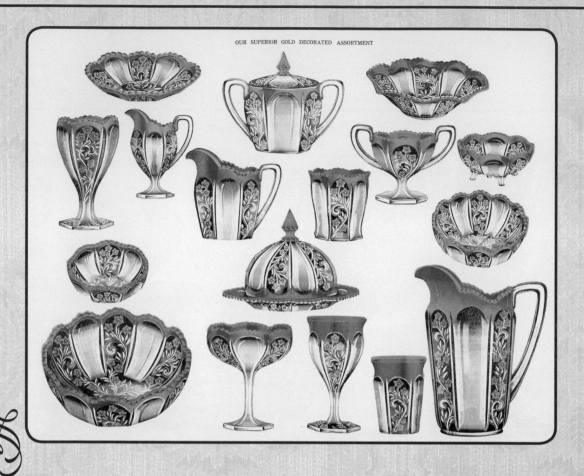

OUR SUPERIOR GOLD DECORATED ASSORTMENT

Pattern: Panelled Heather, OMN: No. 126
Manufacturer: Indiana Glass Company, made in the early 1900s — pattern often mistaken for Jefferson's No. 271 pattern
Date Introduced: c. 1911
Colors Made: Crystal, crystal w/decoration, crystal w/gold, crystal w/ruby stain
Items/Values: Butter dish, crystal, 5½" high, 7⅜" across, $65.00.
Not Shown: Sugar with lid, crystal, $60.00. Creamer, crystal, $40.00. Spooner, crystal, $40.00.

Pattern: Panelled Heather, OMN: No. 126
Manufacturer: Indiana Glass Company, made in the early 1900s — pattern often mistaken for Jefferson's No. 271 Pattern
Date Introduced: c. 1900s
Colors Made: Crystal, crystal w/decoration, crystal w/gold, crystal w/ruby stain
Items/Values: Creamer, rose blush w/gold trim (light), 4¼" high, 6" across, $55.00.
Not Shown: Butter dish, $85.00. Sugar with lid, $70.00. Spooner, $55.00.

OUR IDEAL RUBY AND GOLD DECORATED DINING SET ASSORTMENT

Pattern: Panelled Strawberry, AKA: Indiana's No. 127,
Strawberry with Roman Key
Manufacturer: Indiana Glass Company
Date Introduced: c. 1911
Colors Made: Crystal, crystal w/gold, crystal w/ruby
decoration/gold
Items/Values: Butter dish, $95.00. Sugar with lid, $80.00.
Creamer, $75.00. Spooner, $60.00.
Notes: Values for plain crystal pieces are 20% less than
crystal w/ruby decoration and gold. Values given are for
crystal w/ruby decoration and gold.

Pattern: Panelled Thumbprint, OMN: Famous, Thumbprint Panel
Manufacturer: Co-Operative Flint Glass Company
Date Introduced: c. 1899
Colors Made: Crystal
Items/Values: Butter dish, 5⅜" high, 7⅜" across, $70.00.
Not Shown: Sugar with lid, $55.00. Creamer, $40.00.
Spooner, $40.00.

Pattern: Parachute, AKA: Rabbit Tracks, National No. 600
Manufacturer: National Glass Company
Date Introduced: c. 1901
Colors Made: Crystal
Items/Values: Butter dish, 5¼" high, 7" across, $75.00.
Not Shown: Sugar with lid, $65.00. Creamer, $50.00.
Spooner, $45.00.

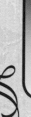

Pattern: Pattee Cross, OMN: U.S. Glass No. 15112
Manufacturer: U.S. Glass Company, made at factory "E," Tarentum, Pennsylvania,
and at factory "B," Pittsburgh, Pennsylvania
Date Introduced: c. 1909
Colors Made: Amethyst flash, crystal, emerald
Items/Values: Spooner, amethyst flash, $50.00. Spooner, crystal, raised lower edge,
3¼" high, 6¼" across, $40.00.
Not Shown: Butter dish, crystal, $60.00. Butter dish, amethyst flash, $75.00. Sugar
with lid, crystal, $45.00. Sugar with lid, amethyst flash, $60.00. Creamer, crystal,
$40.00. Creamer, amethyst flash, $50.00.

Pattern: Pearl, Huntington's, OMN: Pearl
Manufacturer: Huntington Glass Company, Huntington, West Virginia
Date Introduced: c. 1892
Colors Made: Crystal, crystal w/ruby stain (plain and etched)
Items/Values: Butter dish, crystal w/etch, 6¼" high, 6⅜" across, $160.00.
Sugar with lid, crystal w/etch, 7⅝" high, 3½" across, $140.00. Creamer,
crystal w/etch, 5⅝" high, 5⅝" across, $120.00. Spooner, crystal w/etch,
5¼" high, 3" across, $120.00.

Pattern: Pennsylvania, OMN:
U.S. Glass No. 15048 &
15048½ – Pennsylvania.
AKA: Balder, Hand, Kamoni
Manufacturer: U.S. Glass
Company, Pittsburgh,
Pennsylvania, c. 1898 – 1912
Date Introduced: c. 1898
Colors Made: Crystal, crystal
w/gold, crystal w/ruby stain
Reproductions: Crystal
spooner, unmarked
Items/Values: Butter dish,
crystal w/gold, 5½" high, 8" across, $95.00. Sugar with lid, crystal w/gold, 6" high, 4¾" across,
$90.00. Creamer, crystal w/gold, 3¾" high, 5" across, $75.00. Spooner, crystal
w/gold, 4" high, 4" across, $75.00. Cruet with original stopper, crystal, 6⅜" high, $85.00.
Not Shown: Butter dish, crystal, $85.00. Sugar with lid, crystal, $75.00. Creamer, crystal, $65.00.
Spooner, crystal, $60.00. Cruet with original stopper, crystal w/gold, $110.00.

Pattern: Pillow and Sunburst, AKA: Elite
Manufacturer: Westmoreland Specialty Glass Company, Grapeville, Pennsylvania
Date Introduced: c. 1897
Colors Made: Crystal
Items/Values: Butter dish, 3⅞" high, 5⅜" across, patent date Feb. 25, 1876, "W.S. Company" embossed on lid knob, $75.00. Sugar with lid, 5⅛" high, 3⅜" across, $65.00. Creamer with lid (no lid shown), 3½" high, 4¾" across, $65.00.
Notes: Creamer and sugar were sold with mustard enclosed.

Pattern: Pillow Encircled, OMN: Model No. 857. AKA: Midway
Manufacturer: Model Flint Glass Company, c. 1889; Cambridge Glass Company, c. 1901
Date Introduced: c. 1889
Colors Made: Crystal, crystal w/decoration, crystal w/etch, crystal w/frost, crystal w/ruby stain
Items/Values: Creamer, crystal, 4½" high 4⅞" across, $30.00.
Not Shown: Butter dish, $60.00. Sugar with lid, $40.00. Spooner, $30.00.

Pattern: Pineapple & Fan (U.S. Glass), OMN: U.S. Glass No. 15041. AKA: Cube with Fan, Holbrook
Manufacturer: U.S. Glass Company, Pittsburgh, Pennsylvania, factory "A" - factory "GP"
Date Introduced: c. 1895
Colors Made: Crystal, crystal w/gold
Items/Values: Butter dish, crystal, 5½" high, 7¾" across, $45.00. Celery vase, crystal w/gold, 6⅝" high, 3¾" across, $35.00.
Not Shown: Butter dish, crystal w/gold, $50.00. Sugar with lid, crystal, $40.00. Sugar with lid, crystal w/gold, $45.00. Creamer, crystal, $35.00. Creamer, crystal w/gold, $40.00. Spooner, crystal, $35.00. Spooner, crystal w/gold, $40.00. Celery vase, crystal, $30.00.

Pattern: Pioneer's No. 21, AKA: Bull's Eye, Arrowhead
Manufacturer: Dithridge and Company
Date Introduced: c. 1891
Colors Made: Crystal, crystal w/amber, crystal w/ruby stain
Items/Values: Butter dish, crystal w/amber, $150.00.
Not Shown: Sugar with lid, crystal w/amber, $100.00.
  Creamer, crystal w/amber, $100.00. Spooner, crystal
  w/amber, $90.00.

Pattern: Pioneer's No. 21, AKA: Bull's Eye, Arrowhead
Manufacturer: Dithridge and Company
Date Introduced: c. 1891
Colors Made: Crystal, crystal w/amber, crystal w/ruby stain
Items/Values: Castor set, crystal, 9⅛" high, 6½" across bottom
  of base, cruet doesn't have original stopper, $125.00.

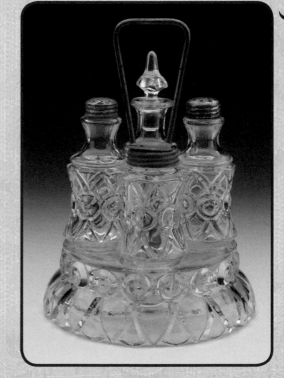

Pattern: Plain Band
Manufacturer: A.H. Heisey & Company, Newark, Ohio
Date Introduced: c. 1897
Colors Made: Crystal, crystal w/decoration
Items/Values: Butter dish, crystal w/gold band
  engraving, 5⅞" high, 7⅜" across, $100.00.
Not Shown: Sugar with lid, $70.00. Creamer, $45.00.
  Spooner, $40.00.

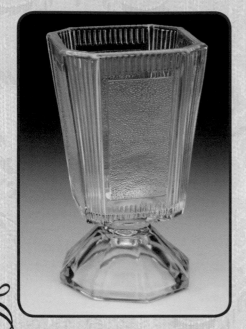

Pattern: Pleat and Panel, OMN: Derby
Manufacturer: Bryce Brothers, Pittsburgh, Pennsylvania, c. 1882; U.S. Glass Company, Pittsburgh, Pennsylvania, c. after 1891
Date Introduced: c. 1882
Colors Made: Crystal
Reproductions: Goblet, 7" square plate, crystal, unmarked
Items/Values: Spooner, 5⅝" high, 3⅛" across, $35.00.
Not Shown: Butter dish, low foot, tab handles, 6" square, $260.00. Butter dish, flat, w/o handles, $150.00. Sugar with lid, $160.00. Creamer, $40.00.

Pattern: Plume, OMN: Adams' No. 3
Manufacturer: Adams & Company, Pittsburgh, Pennsylvania, c. 1874; U.S. Glass Company, Pittsburgh, Pennsylvania, at factory "A," c. 1891
Date Introduced: c. 1874
Colors Made: Crystal, crystal w/ruby stain (plain or w/gold)
Reproductions: Barrel and goblet by L.G. Wright, in crystal or crystal w/frost
Items/Values: Butter dish, crystal, 6" high, 6¾" across, $95.00. Sugar with lid, crystal, 7¼" high, 3¾" across, $110.00. Creamer, crystal, 5" high, 5" across, $75.00. Spooner, crystal, 4⅝" high, 3⁷⁄₁₆" across, $60.00.

Pattern: Pointed Jewel, OMN: U.S. Glass No. 15006. AKA: Long Diamond, Pointed Jewels, Spear Point

Manufacturer: Columbia Glass Company, Findlay, Ohio, c. 1888; U.S. Glass Company, Pittsburgh, Pennsylvania, factory "J" and factory "N," after c. 1892

Date Introduced: c. 1888

Colors Made: Crystal

Reproductions: Creamer, tankard

Items/Values: Butter dish, 5½" high, 7¼" across, flanged, $95.00. Sugar with lid, 7" high, 4⅝" across, $80.00. Creamer, 5⅜" high, 5" across, $60.00. Spooner, 4¾" high, 3⅜" across, $55.00.

Not Shown: Butter dish, handled, $115.00.

Pattern: Popcorn

Manufacturer: Traditionally attributed to the Boston & Sandwich Glass Company, Sandwich, Massachusetts

Date Introduced: c. late 1860s

Colors Made: Crystal

Items/Values: Butter dish, 5⅜" high, 6⅛" across, $100.00. Sugar with lid, 7⅜" high, 4½" across, $85.00. Creamer, 4¾" high, 5⅜" across, $75.00. Spooner, 4½" high, 3¾" across, $60.00.

Pattern: Portland, OMN: U.S. Glass No. 15121, AKA: U.S. Portland

Manufacturer: U.S. Glass Company, Pittsburgh, Pennsylvania

Date Introduced: c. 1910

Colors Made: Crystal, crystal w/gold

Reproductions: Creamer, nut dish, pickle tray, relish, and sugar with lid by Wheaton-Graff Giftware, Millville, New Jersey, crystal, unmarked

Items/Values: Butter dish, crystal, 5½" high, 8¼" across, $95.00. Sugar with lid, crystal, 6⅜" high, 5⅛" across, $80.00. Creamer, crystal, 4" high, 5¾" across, $50.00. Spooner, crystal, 4⅛" high, 3¾" across, $45.00. Celery vase, crystal, 5¾" high, 4⅝" across, $60.00.

Pattern: Posies and Pods

Manufacturer: Northwood Glass Company, Wheeling, West Virginia

Date Introduced: c. 1905

Colors Made: Crystal, crystal w/decoration, emerald, opalescent (all plain or w/gold)

Items/Values: Butter dish, lid only shown, $175.00.

Not Shown: Sugar with lid, $150.00. Creamer, $135.00. Spooner, $110.00.

Notes: Values for plain crystal pieces are 25% less than emerald. Values given are for emerald w/gold pieces.

Pattern: Post Script
Manufacturer: Tarentum Glass Company
Date Introduced: c. 1905
Colors Made: Crystal, crystal w/gold, crystal w/ruby stain
Items/Values: Butter dish, 5¼" high, 7¾" across, $85.00. Sugar with lid, 5⅝" high, 4⅜" across, $75.00. Creamer, 4¼" high, 5¼" across, $65.00. Spooner, 4⅛" high, 3¾" across, $50.00.
Notes: Values for plain crystal pieces are 10% less than other colors. Values given are for crystal w/gold pieces.

Pattern: Primrose, OMN: Canton No. 10. AKA: Stippled Primrose
Manufacturer: Canton Glass Company, Canton, Ohio
Date Introduced: c. 1885
Colors Made: Amber, apple green, blue, crystal, yellow
Items/Values: Butter dish, crystal, 5⅜" high, 5⅞" across, $75.00.
Not Shown: Sugar with lid, $65.00. Creamer, $55.00. Spooner, $55.00.

Pattern: Queen Anne, AKA: Beaded Man, Neptune, Old Man, Old Man of the Woods, Santa Claus
Manufacturer: LaBelle Glass Company, Bridgeport, Ohio
Date Introduced: c. 1880
Colors Made: Crystal (plain or w/etch)
Items/Values: Butter dish, 6½" high, 6¾" across, $110.00. Sugar with lid, 8⅜" high, 6½" across, $110.00. Creamer, 5⅜" high, 5½" across, $75.00. Spooner, 5⅛" high, 5½" across, $60.00.

Pattern: Question Mark, OMN: Richards & Hartley No. 55. AKA: Oval Loop
Manufacturer: Richards & Hartley Glass Company, Tarentum,
   Pennsylvania, c. 1885; U.S. Glass Company, Pittsburgh, Pennsylvania,
   at factory "F"
Date Introduced: c. 1885
Colors Made: Crystal
Items/Values: Butter dish, 5" high, 6⅞" across, $85.00. Sugar with lid,
   7" high, 3¾" across, $75.00. Creamer, 4½" high, 5½" across, $60.00.
   Spooner, 4⅞" high, 3⅛" across, $65.00.

Pattern: Quintec
Manufacturer: McKee Glass Company
Date Introduced: c. 1910
Colors Made: Crystal
Items/Values: Butter dish, 5³⁄₁₆" high, 7⅜" across, $45.00.
Not Shown: Sugar with lid, $40.00. Creamer, $30.00. Spooner,
   $30.00.

Pattern: Ranson, OMN: Ranson 500
Manufacturer: Riverside Glass Works, Wellsburg,
   West Virginia
Date Introduced: c. 1899
Colors Made: Crystal, emerald, vaseline (all plain or
   w/gold)
Items/Values: Butter dish, vaseline w/gold, 5¼" high, 7¹¹⁄₁₆"
   across, gold band gone from lid, $175.00.
Not Shown: Sugar with lid, vaseline w/gold, $150.00.
   Creamer, vaseline w/gold, $130.00. Spooner, vaseline
   w/gold, $110.00.

Pattern: Red Block, OMN: Bryce No. 175, Captain Kid – 150, Central's No. 881, Central's No. 893, Doyle No. 250, Duncan's No. 328, Eva, Fostoria's No. 140, Pioneer's No. 250, Virginia – 140. AKA: Barreled Block, Clear Block

Manufacturer: Bryce Brothers, Pittsburgh, Pennsylvania; Central Glass Company, Wheeling, West Virginia; Doyle & Company, Pittsburgh, Pennsylvania, c. 1885; Fostoria Glass Company, Fostoria, Ohio, c. 1890; George Duncan & Sons, Pittsburgh, Pennsylvania; Model Flint Glass Works, Albany, Indiana; Pioneer Glass Works, Pittsburgh, Pennsylvania, c. 1890

Date Introduced: c. 1885

Colors Made: Crystal, crystal w/ruby stain

Reproductions: Goblet and wine in colors

Items/Values: Butter dish, 5¼" high, 7½" across handle to handle, $125.00. Sugar with lid, 6¼" high, 6½" across handle to handle, $100.00. Creamer, 4¼" high, 5¼" across, $95.00. Spooner, 4½" high, 2¾" across, $60.00.

Notes: Values for plain crystal pieces are 35% less than pieces w/ruby stain. Values given are for crystal pieces w/ruby stain.

Pattern: Regina

Manufacturer: Co-Operative Flint Glass Company, Beaver Falls, Pennsylvania; Federal Glass, c. 1914

Date Introduced: c. 1902

Colors Made: Crystal, crystal w/gold

Items/Value: Butter dish, crystal, 5¾" high, 7¼" across, $50.00.

Not Shown: Sugar with lid, $40.00. Creamer, $30.00. Spooner, $30.00.

Pattern: Reticulated Cord, OMN: No. 600. AKA: Drum
Manufacturer: O'Hara Glass Company, c. 1885; U.S. Glass Company,
   c. 1891
Date Introduced: c. 1885
Colors Made: Amber, crystal
Items/Values: Butter dish, crystal, 6¼" high, 6⅝" across, $90.00. Sugar
   with lid, crystal, 7⅜" high, 4¾" across, $80.00. Creamer, crystal,
   4⅞" high, 6¾" across, $70.00.
Not Shown: Spooner, crystal, $75.00.

Pattern: Reverse 44, OMN: U.S. Glass No. 15140 – Athenia. AKA: Paneled 44
Manufacturer: U.S. Glass Company, Pittsburgh, Pennsylvania
Date Introduced: c. 1912
Colors Made: Crystal, crystal w/gold, crystal w/platinum band, green stain, maiden's
   blush
Items/Values: Butter dish, crystal w/platinum, 6¼" high, 8" across, $245.00. Spooner,
   crystal w/platinum, 4⅜" high, 6" across handle to handle, $75.00. Jelly compote,
   crystal w/platinum, 6" high, 4½" across, $110.00.
Not Shown: Sugar with lid, crystal w/platinum, $110.00. Creamer, crystal w/platinum,
   $95.00.

Pattern: Reverse Torpedo, OMN: Dalzell No. 490D. AKA: Bull's Eye
   & Diamond Point, Bull's Eye Band, Bull's Eye with Diamond Point,
   Diamonds and Bull's Eye Band, Pointed Bull's Eye
Manufacturer: Dalzell, Gilmore & Leighton Glass Company, Findlay, Ohio
Date Introduced: c. 1890
Colors Made: Crystal, crystal w/etch
Items/Values: Butter dish, crystal w/etch, 5½" high, 7⅜" across, $130.00.
   Sugar with lid, crystal w/etch, 6½" high, 3¾" across, $120.00. Creamer,
   crystal w/etch, 5⅞" high, 4⅝" across, $80.00. Spooner, crystal w/etch,
   4⅝" high, 3⅜" across, $70.00. Celery vase, crystal w/etch, 6" high, 3⅞"
   across, $85.00.

Pattern: Ribbed Droplet Band, OMN: No. 89
Manufacturer: George Duncan and Sons, Pittsburgh,
   Pennsylvania
Date Introduced: c. 1887
Colors Made: Crystal, crystal w/decoration
Items/Values: Butter dish, crystal, 6⅛" high, 7⁵⁄₁₆"
   across, $65.00.
Not Shown: Sugar with lid, $55.00. Creamer, $40.00.
   Spooner, $40.00.

Pattern: Ribbed Ellipse, AKA: Admiral
Manufacturer: J.B. Higbee Glass Company, Bridgeville, Pennsylvania
Date Introduced: c. 1905
Colors Made: Crystal
Items/Values: Butter dish, 5¼" high, 8¼" across, $70.00. Sugar with lid
  (no lid shown), 4⅜" across, $60.00.
Not Shown: Creamer, $40.00. Spooner, $30.00.

Pattern: Ribbon Candy, OMN: U.S.
  Glass No. 1010. AKA: Bryce,
  Double Loop, Figure Eight
Manufacturer: Bryce Brothers,
  Pittsburgh, Pennsylvania, c. 1880s;
  U.S. Glass Company, Pittsburgh,
  Pennsylvania, at factory "B,"
  c. 1891
Date Introduced: c. 1880s
Colors Made: Crystal
Items/Values: Butter dish, flat, 5¼"
  high, 6¼" across, $85.00. Sugar
  with lid, 7⅜" high, 4¼" across,
  $85.00. Creamer, 5⅜" high, 5"
  across, $65.00. Spooner, 5" high,
  3⅜" across, $70.00.
Not Shown: Butter dish, footed,
  $115.00.
Notes: Finial is easy to drop.

Pattern: Richmond (Nickel-Plate), OMN: Nickel-Plate No. 76. AKA: Akron Block, Bars and Buttons

Manufacturer: Nickel-Plate Glass Company, Fostoria, Ohio, U.S. Glass Company, c. 1891

Date Introduced: c. 1889

Colors Made: Crystal, crystal w/ruby stain

Items/Values: Sugar with lid (no lid shown), crystal, 4" across, $100.00. Creamer, crystal, 4⅝" high, 5⅛" across, $65.00. Cruet, crystal, with stopper (not sure if it is original), $75.00.

Not Shown: Butter dish, $145.00. Spooner, $60.00.

Pattern: Rising Sun, OMN: U.S. Glass No. 15110 – Sunshine. AKA: Sunrise

Manufacturer: U.S. Glass Company, Pittsburgh, Pennsylvania

Date Introduced: c. 1908

Colors Made: Original color production: crystal, crystal w/gold and green stain, crystal w/gold and ruby stain; any other color would be considered rare

Items/Values: Butter dish, crystal w/gold and green stain, 5¼" high, 7½" across, $145.00. Creamer, crystal w/gold and green stain, 3½" high, 6" across, $100.00. Spooner, crystal w/gold and green stain, 3⅜" high, 6¾" across, $100.00. Cruet with original stopper, crystal w/green stain, 7" high, 3" across, $175.00.

Not Shown: Sugar with lid, crystal w/gold and green stain, $130.00.

Pattern: Rising Sun, OMN: U.S. Glass No. 15110 – Sunshine. AKA: Sunrise

Manufacturer: U.S. Glass Company, Pittsburgh, Pennsylvania

Date Introduced: c. 1908

Colors Made: Original color production: crystal, crystal w/green or rose stain, crystal w/ruby stain; any other color would be considered rare

Items/Values: Butter dish, crystal w/gold and ruby stain, 5¼" high, 7½" across, $145.00. Sugar with lid, crystal w/gold and ruby stain, 5⅜" high, 7¼" across, $130.00. Creamer, crystal w/gold and ruby stain, 3¼" high, 5½" across, $100.00. Spooner, crystal w/gold and ruby stain, 3⅜" high, 6½" across, $100.00.

Pattern: Roanoke, AKA: Late Sawtooth
Manufacturer: Ripley & Company, Pittsburgh, Pennsylvania, c. 1889; U.S. Glass Company, Pittsburgh, Pennsylvania, at factory "F," c. 1891
Date Introduced: c. 1889
Colors Made: Crystal, crystal w/ruby stain, other colors scarce
Items/Values: Butter dish, crystal, lid only shown, $50.00 (flat), $75.00 (footed).
Not Shown: Sugar with lid (flat), $40.00. Sugar with lid (footed), $55.00. Creamer (flat), $30.00. Creamer (footed), $40.00. Spooner (flat), $20.00. Spooner (footed), $30.00.

Pattern: Robin Hood, OMN: Fostoria No. 603
Manufacturer: Fostoria Glass Company, Moundsville, West Virginia
Date Introduced: c. 1898
Colors Made: Crystal
Items/Values: Butter dish, 5⅝" high, 7⅛" across, $55.00.
Not Shown: Sugar with lid, $45.00. Creamer, $35.00. Spooner, $30.00.

Pattern: Rock Crystal, OMN: Floral Panel
Manufacturer: New Martinsville Glass Manufacturing Company, New Martinsville, West Virginia
Date Introduced: c. 1902
Colors Made: Crystal, crystal w/gold overall
Items/Values: Butter dish, covered in gold, 5¾" high, 7½" across, $200.00. Sugar with lid, covered in gold, 6⅞" high, 4¼" across, $135.00. Creamer, covered in gold, 4⅝" high, 4⅞" across, $100.00. Spooner, covered in gold, 4⅜" high, 3¾" across, $100.00.

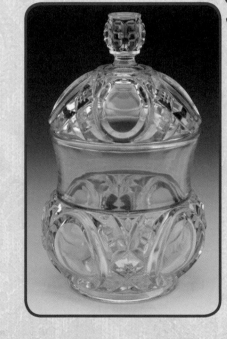

Pattern: Roman Rosette, OMN: U.S. Glass No. 15030
Manufacturer: Bryce, Walker & Company, Pittsburgh, Pennsylvania,
 c. 1875 – 1885; U.S. Glass Company, Pittsburgh, Pennsylvania, at
 factory "A," c. 1894
Date Introduced: c. 1875
Colors Made: Crystal, crystal w/ruby stain
Reproductions: Goblet, crystal, unmarked
Items/Values: Butter dish, crystal, 5⅛" high, 6½" across, $110.00.
 Sugar with lid, crystal, 6¾" high, 4¼" across, $85.00. Creamer,
 crystal, 5⅛" high, 4¾" across, $55.00. Spooner, crystal, 4⅝" high,
 3⅜" across, $55.00.

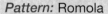

Pattern: Romola
Manufacturer: Robinson Glass Company, c. 1894; Model Flint Glass, c. 1901
Date Introduced: c. 1894
Colors Made: Crystal
Items/Values: Sugar with lid, 7⅛" high, 3¾" across, $50.00.
Not Shown: Butter dish, $60.00. Creamer, $40.00. Spooner, $35.00.

Pattern: Rose Point Band, OMN: No. 153.
 AKA: Waterlily, Clematis,153 Pattern
Manufacturer: Indiana Glass Company, Dunkirk,
 Indiana
Date Introduced: c. 1913
Colors Made: Crystal
Items/Values: Butter dish, 5" high, 7⅜" across,
 $65.00.
Not Shown: Sugar with lid, $50.00. Creamer, $40.00.
 Spooner, $40.00.

Pattern: Sawtoothed Honeycomb, OMN: Steimer's Diamond, Union's Radiant. AKA: Chickenwire, Sawtooth Honeycomb, Serrated Block & Loop

Manufacturer: Steimer Glass Company, Buckhannon, West Virginia, c. 1906; Union Stopper Company, Morgantown, West Virginia, c. 1908

Date Introduced: c. 1906

Colors Made: Crystal, crystal w/gold, crystal w/ruby stain

Items/Values: Butter dish, crystal w/gold, 5½" high, 7½" across, $80.00.

Not Shown: Sugar with lid, crystal w/gold, $70.00. Creamer, crystal w/gold, $60.00. Spooner, crystal w/gold, $50.00.

Pattern: Scalloped Lines, AKA: Scalloped Band

Manufacturer: Sweeney, McCluney & Company, N. Wheeling, West Virginia

Date Introduced: c. 1871

Colors Made: Crystal

Items/Values: Butter dish, 5¹⁄₁₆" high, 6⅛" across, $95.00.

Not Shown: Sugar with lid, $85.00. Creamer, $70.00. Spooner, $65.00.

Pattern: Scalloped Six Point, OMN: Duncan's No. 30. AKA: Divided Medallion with Diamond Cut

Manufacturer: George Duncan's Sons & Company, Washington, Pennsylvania

Date Introduced: c. 1897

Colors Made: Crystal, crystal w/ruby

Items/Values: Butter dish, crystal, 5⅝" high, 8¼" across, $80.00. Cruet with stopper, not original stopper, crystal, 6" high, $80.00.

Not Shown: Sugar with lid, $65.00. Creamer, $50.00. Spooner, $40.00.

Pattern: Scalloped Skirt, AKA: Vogue
Manufacturer: Jefferson Glass Company, Steubenville, Ohio
Date Introduced: c. 1904
Colors Made: Amethyst, blue, blue w/enamel, crystal, crystal w/enamel, green (all plain or w/gold)
Items/Values: Butter dish, blue enameled w/gold trim, 5½" high, 7⅜" across, $125.00. Sugar with lid, blue enameled w/gold trim, 6¾" high, 4½" across, $110.00. Creamer, blue enameled w/gold trim, 4⅜" across, 5¾" across, $95.00. Spooner, blue enameled w/gold trim, 4⁵⁄₁₆" high, 4⅛" across, $80.00.

Pattern: Scroll with Cane Band, OMN: West Virginia's No. 213
Manufacturer: West Virginia Glass Company, Martins Ferry, Ohio
Date Introduced: c. 1895
Colors Made: Crystal, crystal w/amber, crystal w/ruby stain
Items/Values: Butter dish, crystal w/amber stain, 5¾" high, 8" across, $90.00.
Not Shown: Sugar with lid, crystal w/amber stain, $75.00. Creamer, crystal w/amber stain, $60.00. Spooner, crystal w/amber stain, $60.00.

Pattern: Scroll with Flowers
Manufacturer: Unknown
Date Introduced: c. 1880s
Colors Made: Crystal
Items/Values: Butter dish, 4½"
high, 7⅛" across, $80.00. Sugar
with lid, 6¾" high, 5¹⁵⁄₁₆" across,
$75.00. Creamer, 4¾" high, 5⅛"
across, $60.00. Spooner, 4½"
high, 5⅛" across, $50.00.

Pattern: Seedpod, AKA: Olympia
Manufacturer: Riverside Glass Works, Wellsburg,
West Virginia ("Olympia" in honor of Admiral
Dewey's flagship)
Date Introduced: c. 1898
Colors Made: Cobalt w/gold, crystal, crystal w/gold,
emerald w/gold
Items/Values: Butter dish, cobalt w/gold, 5⅛" high,
7⅝" across, $155.00. Sugar with lid, cobalt
w/gold, 6⅞" high, 3¾" across, $120.00. Creamer,
cobalt w/gold, 5⅞" high, 4⅞" across, $85.00.
Spooner, cobalt w/gold, 4¾" high, 3½" across,
$65.00.

Pattern: Seedpod, AKA: Olympia
Manufacturer: Riverside Glass Works, Wellsburg, West
Virginia ("Olympia" in honor of Admiral Dewey's flagship)
Date Introduced: c. 1898
Colors Made: Cobalt w/gold, crystal, crystal w/gold,
emerald w/gold
Items/Values: Butter dish, crystal w/gold, 5¼" high, 7⅝"
across, $110.00.
Not Shown: Sugar with lid, crystal w/gold, $90.00. Creamer,
crystal w/gold, $80.00. Spooner, crystal w/gold, $65.00.

Pattern: Serrated Rib and Fine Cut
Manufacturer: Unknown
Date Introduced: c. 1900s
Colors Made: Crystal
Items/Values: Butter dish, 5¾" high, 8⅛" across, $60.00.
Not Shown: Sugar with lid, $50.00. Creamer, $40.00. Spooner, $35.00.

Pattern: Sextec
Manufacturer: McKee Glass Company
Date Introduced: c. 1906
Colors Made: Crystal, crystal w/gold
Items/Values: Butter dish, crystal, 4⅞" high, 7⅞" across, $75.00. Sugar with lid, crystal w/gold, 4⅞" high, 8¼" across handle to handle, $75.00.
Not Shown: Butter dish, crystal w/gold, $85.00. Sugar with lid, crystal, $65.00. Creamer, crystal, $50.00. Creamer, crystal w/gold, $55.00. Spooner, crystal, $35.00. Spooner, crystal w/gold, $40.00.

Pattern: Sheaf and Diamond, AKA: Diamond with Double Fans, Banded Stalks
Manufacturer: Bryce, Higbee & Company, 1899 – 1905; J.B. Higbee Glass Company, 1907
Date Introduced: c. 1899
Colors Made: Crystal
Items/Values: Butter dish, 5¾" high, 6¾" across, $65.00. Celery vase, 7⅞" high, 4¼" across, $50.00.
Not Shown: Sugar with lid, $55.00. Creamer, $40.00. Spooner, $35.00.

Pattern: Shell and Tassel, OMN: Duncan No. 555. AKA: Hedlin Shell, Shell and Spike, Shell and Tassel – Square

Manufacturer: George A. Duncan & Sons, Pittsburgh, Pennsylvania, designed by Augustus H. Heisey and patented July 26, 1881, in two versions: item with frosted corner shells (U.S. Patent No. 12371) and item with crystal corner shells (U.S. Patent No. 12372)

Date Introduced: c. 1881

Colors Made: Amber, blue, canary yellow, crystal

Reproductions: Butter with cover, footed, goblet, unmarked, by L.G. Wright Glass Company, New Martinsville, West Virginia

Items/Values: Butter dish, round with collared base and frosted dog finial, 6½" high, 7⅞" across, $250.00.

Not Shown: Sugar with lid, $195.00. Creamer, $80.00. Spooner, $75.00.

Pattern: Sheraton

Manufacturer: Bryce, Higbee & Company, Pittsburgh, Pennsylvania

Date Introduced: c. 1885

Colors Made: Amber, blue, crystal

Items/Values: Butter dish, crystal, 4¾" high, 6¼" across, $85.00. Sugar with lid, crystal, 7⅜" high, 4¼" across, $75.00. Creamer, crystal, 5⅝" high, 5⅛" across, $55.00. Spooner, crystal, 4¾" high, 3⅜" across, $55.00.

Pattern: Shoshone, OMN: U.S. Glass No. 15046 – Victor. AKA: Blazing Pinwheels, Floral Diamond

Manufacturer: U.S. Glass Company, Pittsburgh, Pennsylvania

Date Introduced: c. 1895

Colors Made: Crystal, crystal w/amber, crystal w/gold, crystal w/ruby, emerald

Items/Values: Butter dish, crystal w/gold, 5⅝" high, 7⅞" across, $75.00. Cruet with original stopper, crystal, 7¼" high, 4" across, $95.00.

Not Shown: Butter dish, crystal, $65.00. Sugar with lid, crystal, $60.00. Sugar with lid, crystal w/gold, $70.00. Creamer, crystal, $45.00. Creamer, crystal w/gold, $50.00. Spooner, crystal, $50.00. Spooner, crystal w/gold, $55.00. Cruet with original stopper, crystal w/gold, $110.00.

Pattern: Shrine, OMN: Orient. AKA: Jewel with Moon and Star, Jeweled Moon and Star, Little Shrine, Moon and Star with Waffle
Manufacturer: Beatty-Brady Glass Company, Dunkirk, Indiana, c. 1896; Indiana Glass Company, Dunkirk, Indiana, c. 1904
Date Introduced: c. 1896
Colors Made: Crystal
Items/Values: Butter dish, 5⅝" high, 7" across, $110.00.
Not Shown: Sugar with lid, $95.00. Creamer, $65.00. Spooner, $50.00.

Pattern: Silver Queen, AKA: Elmino
Manufacturer: Ripley & Company, Pittsburgh, Pennsylvania, c. 1890; U.S. Glass Company, factory "F," Pittsburgh, Pennsylvania
Date Introduced: c. 1890
Colors Made: Crystal, crystal w/etch
Items/Values: Butter dish, crystal w/etch, 6" high, 7¼" across, $65.00.
Not Shown: Butter dish, crystal, $40.00. Sugar with lid, crystal, $35.00. Sugar with lid, crystal w/etch, $55.00. Creamer, crystal, $30.00. Creamer, crystal w/etch, $40.00. Spooner, crystal, $30.00. Spooner, crystal w/etch, $40.00.

Pattern: Simplicity, AKA: Pattern 705, Engraving No. 189
Manufacturer: Central Glass Company, Wheeling, West Virginia
Date Introduced: Unknown
Colors Made: Crystal, crystal w/etch
Items/Values: Butter dish, crystal w/etch, 7½" high, 7¾" across, $160.00. Sugar with lid, crystal w/etch, 9¼" high, 6¼" across, $135.00. Creamer, crystal w/etch, 7" high, 5¼" across, $110.00. Spooner, crystal w/etch, 6⅝" high, 5½" across, $100.00.

Pattern: Skilton, AKA: Early Oregon, Richards & Hartley's Oregon
Manufacturer: Richards & Hartley Glass Company, Tarentum,
   Pennsylvania, c. 1890; U.S. Glass Company after 1891
Date Introduced: c. 1890
Colors Made: Crystal, crystal w/ruby stain
Items/Values: Butter dish, crystal, 5⅜" high, 7¹⁄₁₆" across, $85.00. Milk
   pitcher, crystal, 6" high, 6¾" across, $85.00.
Not Shown: Sugar with lid, $60.00. Creamer, $45.00. Spooner, $40.00.

Pattern: Slewed Horseshoe, OMN: U.S. Glass No. 15111.
   AKA: Radiant Daisy, U.S. Peacock
Manufacturer: U.S. Glass Company, Glassport,
   Pennsylvania
Date Introduced: c. 1908
Colors Made: Crystal, iodized c. 1930s
Items/Values: Berry sugar, open, crystal, 3¹⁵⁄₁₆" high, 7"
   across, $25.00
Not Shown: Butter dish, $75.00. Sugar with lid, $60.00.
   Creamer, $50.00. Spooner, $30.00.

Pattern: Snail, OMN: Duncan's No. 360 Ware. AKA: Compact, Double Snail, Idaho, Small Comet

Manufacturer: George Duncan & Sons, Pittsburgh, Pennsylvania, c. 1891; U.S. Glass Company, Pittsburgh, Pennsylvania, at factory "D," later produced at factory "P"

Date Introduced: c. 1891

Colors Made: Crystal, crystal w/etch, crystal w/ruby stain

Reproductions: Tankard water pitcher

Items/Values: Butter dish, 6¼" high, 8" across, $145.00. Sugar with lid, crystal, 7⅜" high, 4¼" across, $115.00. Spooner, crystal, 4⅝" high, 3½" across, $55.00.

Not Shown: Creamer, $90.00.

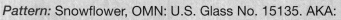

Pattern: Snowflower, OMN: U.S. Glass No. 15135. AKA: Flower Fan

Manufacturer: U.S. Glass Company

Date Introduced: c. 1912

Colors Made: Crystal

Items/Value: Butter dish, 5½" high, 8¼" across, $65.00

Not Shown: Sugar with lid, $50.00. Creamer, $40.00. Spooner, $35.00.

Pattern: Solar, OMN: U.S. Glass No. 15116.
  AKA: Feathered Swirl
Manufacturer: U. S. Glass Company
Date Introduced: c. 1908
Colors Made: Crystal
Items/Values: Creamer, 5⅜" high, 6" across, $40.00.
Not Shown: Butter dish, $60.00. Sugar with lid,
  $50.00. Spooner, $35.00.

Pattern: Spatula, OMN: Tarentum No. 240
Manufacturer: Tarentum Glass Company, Tarentum, Pennsylvania
Date Introduced: c. 1907
Colors Made: Crystal, crystal w/gold, crystal w/ruby stain
Items/Values: Butter dish, crystal w/gold trim, 5⅞" high, 7¾" across,
  $65.00. Sugar with lid, crystal w/gold trim, 6½" high, 4¼" across,
  $50.00. Creamer, crystal w/gold trim, 3¾" high, 5¼" across, $40.00.
  Spooner, crystal w/gold trim, 3¹⁵⁄₁₆" high, 3⅝" across, $40.00.

Pattern: Spirea Band, OMN: Earl. AKA: Nailhead Variant, Spirea, Square and Dot, Squared Dot
Manufacturer: Bryce, Higbee & Company, Pittsburgh, Pennsylvania
Date Introduced: c. 1885
Colors Made: Amber, blue, crystal, vaseline
Items/Values: Sugar with lid (no lid shown), amber, 4¼" across, $60.00.
Not Shown: Butter dish, amber, $65.00. Creamer, amber, $50.00. Spooner, amber, $35.00.

Pattern: Spirea Band, OMN: Earl. AKA: Nailhead Variant, Spirea, Square and Dot, Squared Dot
Manufacturer: Bryce, Higbee & Company, Pittsburgh, Pennsylvania
Date Introduced: c. 1885
Colors Made: Amber, blue, crystal, vaseline
Items/Values: Butter dish, blue, 4⅝" high, 7" across, $80.00.
Not Shown: Sugar with lid, blue, $70.00. Creamer, blue, $65.00. Spooner, blue, $70.00.

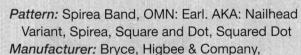

Pattern: Sprig, OMN: Bryce's Royal. AKA: Indian Tree, Paneled Sprig
Manufacturer: Bryce, Higbee & Company, Pittsburgh, Pennsylvania
Date Introduced: c. 1885
Colors Made: Crystal
Items/Values: Sugar with lid, 8⅜" high, 6⅝" across, $95.00. Creamer,
   5⅝" high, 5¼" across, $65.00. Spooner, 5⅜" high, 5⅜" across, $50.00.
Not Shown: Butter dish, $115.00.

Close-up of Sprig design.

Pattern: Squat Pineapple, AKA: Lone Star, Gem
Manufacturer: McKee Brothers, c. 1898; National Glass, c. 1902;
  Federal Glass, c. 1914
Date Introduced: c. 1898
Colors Made: Crystal, emerald
Items/Values: Sugar with lid, crystal, 6⅜" high, 5⅛" across, $65.00.
Not Shown: Butter dish, $80.00. Creamer, $60.00. Spooner, $45.00.

Pattern: Star and Crescent, OMN: U.S. Glass No. 15108.
  AKA: Festoons and Sunbursts
Manufacturer: U.S. Glass Company (King; Ripley)
Date Introduced: c. 1908
Colors Made: Crystal, crystal w/gold
Items/Values: Butter dish, 5½" high, 7⁵⁄₁₆" across, $65.00.
Not Shown: Sugar with lid, $65.00. Creamer, $50.00.
  Spooner, $40.00.
Notes: Values for plain crystal pieces are 10% less than
  other pieces. Values given are for crystal w/gold pieces.

Pattern: Star Band, AKA: Bosworth
Manufacturer: Indiana Glass
  Company of Dunkirk, Indiana
Date Introduced: c. 1915
Colors Made: Crystal, crystal
  w/gold, crystal w/ruby stain
Items/Values: Butter dish, 5⅜"
  high, 7¼" across, $85.00. Sugar
  with lid, 6½" high, 6⅝" across,
  $70.00. Creamer, 4½" high, 5½"
  across spout to handle, $65.00.
  Spooner, 4⅜" high, 3½" across,
  $65.00.
Notes: Values for plain crystal
  pieces are 10% less than
  crystal w/gold. Values given
  are for crystal w/gold pieces.

Pattern: Star in Bull's Eye, OMN: U.S. Glass No. 15092
Manufacturer: U.S. Glass Company, Pittsburgh, Pennsylvania
Date Introduced: c. 1905
Colors Made: Crystal, crystal w/gold, crystal w/maiden blush, ruby stain
Items/Values: Butter dish, 4⅞" high, 8⅛" across, $75.00.
Not Shown: Sugar with lid, $60.00. Creamer, $50.00. Spooner, $40.00.
Notes: Values for plain crystal pieces are 10% less than crystal w/gold pieces. Values given are for crystal w/gold pieces.

Pattern: Star in Diamond, OMN: Gillinder No. 414. AKA: U.S. Glass No. 414, Barred Star, Spartan
Manufacturer: Gillinder & Sons, c. 1880s; U.S. Glass Company, c. 1891
Date Introduced: c. 1880s
Colors Made: Crystal
Items/Values: Sugar with lid (no lid shown), 4" across, $55.00.
Not Shown: Butter dish, $65.00. Creamer, $40.00. Spooner, $35.00.

Pattern: Star of David, OMN: No. 500, Wetzel
Manufacturer: New Martinsville Glass Manufacturing Company, New Martinsville, West Virginia
Date Introduced: c. 1905
Colors Made: Crystal (plain or w/gold), crystal w/ruby stain
Items/Values: Butter dish, 6" high, 8" across, $110.00. Sugar with lid, 7" high, 4⅝" across, $100.00. Creamer, 4⅝" high, 5⅞" across, $80.00. Spooner, 4⅛" high, 4⅛" across, $70.00.
Notes: Values for plain crystal pieces are 10% less than crystal w/gold. Values given are for crystal w/gold pieces.

Pattern: Starred Block, AKA: Daisy and Button Petticoat, Daisy Band, Daisy and Button with Petticoat Band
Manufacturer: Dalzell Brothers and Gilmore, c. 1885; Dalzell, Gilmore & Leighton, c. 1888
Date Introduced: c. 1885
Colors Made: Crystal
Items/Values: Spooner, $4^{11}/_{16}$" high, $3^9/_{16}$" across, $35.00.
Not Shown: Butter dish, $55.00. Sugar with lid, $45.00. Creamer, $40.00.

Pattern: Starred Loop, OMN: No. "45"
Manufacturer: George Duncan's Sons & Company, Washington, Pennsylvania, 1899; Duncan & Miller Glass Company, 1900 – 1955
Date Introduced: c. 1899
Colors Made: Crystal, crystal w/gold
Items/Values: Celery vase, crystal, $5^7/_8$" high, $3^3/_8$" across, $45.00.
Not Shown: Butter dish, $65.00. Sugar with lid, $45.00. Creamer, $45.00. Spooner, $40.00.

Pattern: Stippled Daisy
Manufacturer: Unknown
Date Introduced: c. 1880s
Colors Made: Crystal
Items/Values: Butter dish, stippled, $4^5/_{16}$" high, $6^3/_8$" across, $45.00. Creamer, stippled, $4^1/_2$" high, $4^5/_8$" across, $35.00. Spooner, stippled, $4^5/_8$" high, $3^1/_2$" across, $30.00.
Not Shown: Sugar with lid, $40.00.

Pattern: Stippled Dart & Balls
Manufacturer: Unknown
Date Introduced: c. 1890
Colors Made: Crystal
Items/Values: Spooner (spill), stippled around design, 3⁷⁄₈"
   high, 3³⁄₈" across, $30.00.
Not Shown: Butter dish, $40.00. Sugar with lid, $35.00.
   Creamer, $30.00.

Pattern: Stippled Double Loop, AKA: Double Loop
Manufacturer: Unknown
Date Introduced: c. 1870s
Colors Made: Crystal w/stippling
Items/Values: Butter dish, 4½" high, 6³⁄₈" across,
   $95.00. Creamer, 4⁵⁄₈" high, 5½" across, $65.00.
   Spooner, 4⁵⁄₈" high, 3½" across, $50.00.
Not Shown: Sugar with lid, $110.00.

Pattern: Stippled Forget-Me-Not, AKA: Dot, Forget-Me-Not in Snow
Manufacturer: Findlay Flint Glass Company, Findlay, Ohio
Date Introduced: c. 1890
Colors Made: Amber, blue, crystal, opal, white
Items/Values: Spooner, crystal, 4⁷⁄₈" high, 3½" across, $60.00.
Not Shown: Butter dish, $130.00. Sugar with lid, $100.00. Creamer, $80.00.

Pattern: Sydney, OMN: No. 1333
Manufacturer: Fostoria Glass Company,
   Moundsville, West Virginia
Date Introduced: c. 1905
Colors Made: Crystal
Items/Values: Butter dish, 5⅜" high, 8" across,
   $85.00.
Not Shown: Sugar with lid, $70.00. Creamer,
   $60.00. Spooner, $55.00.

Pattern: Sylvan, AKA: Overall Diamond, English Hobnail Variant
Manufacturer: Fostoria Glass Company, Moundsville,
   West Virginia
Date Introduced: c. 1902
Colors Made: Crystal, crystal w/gold
Items/Values: Creamer, 4¹¹⁄₁₆" high, 5¼" across, $50.00.
Not Shown: Butter dish, $75.00. Sugar with lid, $65.00.
   Spooner, $45.00.
Notes: Values for plain crystal pieces are 10% less than crystal
   w/gold pieces. Values given are for crystal w/gold pieces.

Pattern: Tacoma, OMN: Model No. 907.
   AKA: Jeweled Diamond and Fan, Triple X
Manufacturer: Greensburg Glass Company,
   Greensburg, Pennsylvania, c. 1894;
   Model Flint Glass Company, Albany,
   Indiana, c. 1900
Date Introduced: c. 1894
Colors Made: Crystal, crystal w/amber
   stain, crystal w/ruby stain
Items/Values: Cruet, small, with stopper
   (no stopper shown), 4⅞" high, hint of sun
   purple, $75.00. Pickle jar, with cover,
   crystal, 6" high, 3½" across, $150.00.
Not Shown: Butter dish, $85.00. Sugar
   with lid, $70.00. Creamer, $55.00.
   Spooner, $45.00. Cruet, large, with
   original stopper, $85.00.

Pattern: Tarentum's Atlanta, AKA: Royal Crystal, Diamond and Teardop, Shining Diamonds
Manufacturer: Tarentum Glass Company, Tarentum, Pennsylvania
Date Introduced: c.1894
Colors Made: Crystal, crystal w/ruby stain
Reproductions: Cake stand
Items/Values: Butter dish, crystal w/ruby stain, 5¾" high, 7¾" across, $140.00. Spooner, crystal w/ruby stain, 5" high, 3⅛" across, $75.00.
Not Shown: Sugar with lid, crystal w/ruby stain, $125.00. Creamer, crystal w/ruby stain, $85.00.

Pattern: Tarentum's Virginia
Manufacturer: Tarentum Glass Company, Tarentum, Pennsylvania
Date Introduced: c. 1895
Colors Made: Crystal, crystal w/ruby stain
Items/Values: Butter dish, crystal, 6" high, 7⅜" across, $75.00. Spooner, crystal, 4⅛" high, 3" across, $45.00. Shaker, 2¾" high, $25.00.
Not Shown: Sugar with lid, $60.00. Creamer, $45.00.

Pattern: Teepee, OMN: Duncan No. 128 – Arizona. AKA: Nemesis, Wigwam
Manufacturer: George Duncan's Sons & Company, Washington, Pennsylvania
Date Introduced: c. 1896
Colors Made: Crystal, crystal w/ruby stain
Items/Values: Sugar with lid (no lid shown), crystal, 3¾" across, $70.00. Cruet with original stopper (no stopper shown), crystal, $90.00. Toothpick holder, crystal, 2⅜" high, 2" across, $45.00.
Not Shown: Butter dish, $85.00. Creamer, $55.00. Spooner, $40.00.

Pattern: Tennessee, OMN: U.S. Glass No. 15064 – Tennessee. AKA: Jewel and Crescent, Jeweled Rose(s), Scrolls with Bull's Eye
Manufacturer: U.S. Glass Company, Pittsburgh, Pennsylvania
Date Introduced: c. 1899
Colors Made: Crystal, crystal w/decoration
Items/Values: Butter dish, crystal, lid only shown, $115.00. Creamer, crystal, 4¼" high, 5⁵⁄₁₆" across, $75.00.
Not Shown: Sugar with lid, $100.00. Spooner, $55.00.

Pattern: Teutonic, AKA: Long Star, IHC
Manufacturer: McKee & Brothers,
   Jeannette, Pennsylvania, 1888 – 1900
Date Introduced: c. 1894
Colors Made: Crystal
Items/Values: Butter dish, lid only shown,
   $60.00. Celery vase, 6¼" high, 3⅞"
   across, $45.00.
Not Shown: Sugar with lid, $45.00.
   Creamer, $35.00. Spooner, $35.00.

Pattern: Texas, OMN: U.S. Glass No. 15067 – Texas.
   AKA: Loop with Stippled Panels
Manufacturer: U.S. Glass Company
Date Introduced: c. 1900
Colors Made: Crystal, crystal w/gold, crystal w/rose
   stain (plain or w/gold)
Reproductions: Some colors
Items/Values: Toothpick holder, crystal w/gold, $75.00.
Not Shown: Butter dish, $185.00. Sugar with lid,
   $170.00. Creamer, $150.00. Spooner, $130.00.
Notes: Values for plain crystal pieces are 10% less
   than crystal w/gold. Values given are for crystal w/gold
   pieces.

Pattern: Thistleblow, OMN:
   Kokomo-Jenkins No. 514.
   AKA: Panelled Iris
Manufacturer: Kokomo
   Glass Manufacturing
   Company
Date Introduced: c. 1905
Colors Made: Crystal
Items/Values: Butter dish,
   5½" high, 7⁷⁄₁₆" across,
   $55.00. Sugar with lid
   (no lid shown), 6¾" across,
   $50.00. Creamer, 4½" high,
   5⅝" across, $40.00.
Not Shown: Spooner,
   $40.00.

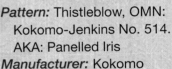

Pattern: Thread Band

Manufacturer: Duncan and Miller Glass Company, Washington, Pennsylvania

Date Introduced: c. late teens through 1920s

Colors Made: Crystal, decorated

Items/Values: Butter dish, crystal w/gold and green bands, 6" high, 7⅛" across, $60.00. Sugar with lid, crystal w/gold and green bands, 6" high, 6¼" across, $50.00. Creamer, crystal w/gold and green bands, 3¾" high, 4¹³⁄₁₆" across, $40.00. Spooner, crystal w/gold and green bands, 3½" high, 5½" across, $40.00.

Notes: Values for plain crystal pieces are 10% less than decorated pieces. Values given are for decorated pieces.

Pattern: Three Panel, OMN: Richards & Hartley No. 25. AKA: Button and Buckle, Paneled Thousand Eye, Thousand Eye Three Panel

Manufacturer: Richards & Hartley Glass Company, Tarentum, Pennsylvania, c. 1880s; U.S. Glass Company, Pittsburgh, Pennsylvania, at factory "E," c. 1891

Date Introduced: c. 1880s

Colors Made: Amber, blue, canary, crystal

Items/Values: Butter dish, flanged lid, 5⅜" high, 5⅝" across, $95.00. Sugar with lid, 7" high, 4¼" across, $80.00. Creamer, 5¼" high, 5½" across, $65.00. Spooner, 5¼" high, 3½" across, $45.00.

Notes: Values for plain crystal pieces are 10% less than amber pieces. Values given are for amber pieces.

Pattern: Three-In-One, OMN: Imperial No. 1. AKA: Fancy Diamonds
Manufacturer: Imperial Glass Company, Bellaire, Ohio
Date Introduced: c. 1902
Colors Made: Crystal
Items/Values: Butter dish, lid only shown, $80.00. Syrup with lid, crystal, 7" high, $100.00.
Not Shown: Sugar with lid, $65.00. Creamer, $50.00. Spooner, $40.00.

Pattern: Thumbnail, OMN: Duncan & Miller No. 73. AKA: Flat to Round Panel
Manufacturer: Duncan & Miller Glass Company, Washington, Pennsylvania
Date Introduced: c. 1905
Colors Made: Crystal, crystal w/gold, crystal w/ruby (plain or w/gold)
Items/Values: Butter dish, 6½" high, 7¾" across, $95.00. Sugar with lid, 7¼" high, 4¼" across, $85.00. Creamer, 4½" high, 5¼" across, $75.00. Spooner, 4⅝" high, 3½" across, $60.00.
Notes: Values for plain crystal pieces are 10% less than crystal w/gold. Values given are for crystal w/gold pieces.

Pattern: Tidal, AKA: Florida Palm, Perfection
Manufacturer: Bryce, Higbee & Company
Date Introduced: c. 1900
Colors Made: Crystal
Items/Values: Sugar with lid, 7⅝" high, 4⅝" across, $65.00. Spooner, 4½" high, 3⅞" across, $40.00.
Not Shown: Butter dish, $80.00. Creamer, $50.00.

Pattern: Toltec
Manufacturer: McKee & Brothers Glass Company
Date Introduced: c. 1903
Colors Made: Crystal
Items/Values: Butter dish, 4¼" high, 7" across, $75.00. Sugar with lid, 7" high, 4½" across, $60.00. Creamer, 4¾" high, 5⅝" across, $50.00. Spooner, 4¼" high, 4⅛" across, $45.00. Cruet, with original stopper, 5⅝" high, $85.00.
Notes: Trademark "Pres-Cut" on most pieces.

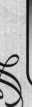

Pattern: Torpedo, OMN: Thompson's No. 17. AKA: Fisheye, Pigmy
Manufacturer: Thompson Glass Company, Uniontown, Pennsylvania
Date Introduced: c. 1889
Colors Made: Crystal, crystal w/ruby stain (plain or engraved)
Items/Values: Butter dish, crystal, 6½" high, 5⅞" across, $95.00. Creamer, crystal, 6¾" high, 4¾" across, $80.00. Spooner, crystal, 5³⁄₁₆" high, 3½" across. Celery vase, crystal, 6⁹⁄₁₆" high, 3½" across, $65.00.
Not Shown: Sugar with lid, $110.00.

Pattern: Triple Triangle, OMN: Doyle No. 76. AKA: Triple Triangle – Red Top, Pillar and Cut Diamond

Manufacturer: Doyle & Company, Pittsburgh, Pennsylvania, c. 1880; U.S. Glass Company, Pittsburgh, Pennsylvania, at factory "D," c. 1891 – 1895

Date Introduced: c. 1880

Colors Made: Crystal, crystal w/ruby stain (plain or w/etch)

Reproductions: Goblet and wine, unmarked

Items/Values: Butter dish, crystal w/ruby stain, 5¼" high, 8" across, $155.00. Sugar with lid, crystal w/ruby stain, 6½" high, 7¼" across, $150.00. Creamer, crystal w/ruby stain, 4⅛" high, 5½" across, $95.00. Spooner, crystal w/ruby stain, 4¼" high, 5½" across, $110.00.

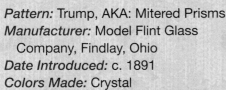

Pattern: Trump, AKA: Mitered Prisms

Manufacturer: Model Flint Glass Company, Findlay, Ohio

Date Introduced: c. 1891

Colors Made: Crystal

Items/Values: Butter dish, 6" high, 7¼" across, $95.00. Sugar with lid, 6¾" high, 7¼" across, $80.00. Creamer, 4⅜" high, 5⅜" across, $60.00. Spooner, 4¼" high, 5¾" across, $50.00. Celery vase, 6¼" high, 7⅛" across, $60.00.

Pattern: Truncated Cube, OMN: Thompson No. 77

Manufacturer: Thompson Glass Company, Uniontown, Pennsylvania

Date Introduced: c. 1894

Colors Made: Crystal, crystal w/ruby stain (plain or etched)

Items/Values: Celery vase, 6⅜" high, 4" across, $100.00.

Not Shown: Butter dish, $145.00. Sugar with lid, $130.00. Creamer, $95.00. Spooner, $80.00.

Notes: Values for plain crystal pieces are 30% less than crystal w/ruby stain. Values given are for crystal w/ruby stain pieces.

Pattern: Tulip with Sawtooth, OMN: Bryce No. 1 – Tulip
Manufacturer: Bryce, McKee & Company
Date Introduced: c. 1860s
Colors Made: Crystal, milk opalescent
Reproductions: Goblet, wine (non-flint)
Items/Values: Butter dish, crystal, non-flint, 5⅛" high, 5⅞" across, $60.00.
Not Shown: Butter dish, flint, $155.00. Sugar with lid, flint, $155.00. Sugar with lid, non-flint, $50.00. Creamer, flint, $125.00. Creamer, non-flint, $90.00. Spooner, flint, $125.00. Spooner, non-flint, $50.00.

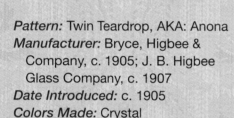

Pattern: Twin Teardrop, AKA: Anona
Manufacturer: Bryce, Higbee & Company, c. 1905; J. B. Higbee Glass Company, c. 1907
Date Introduced: c. 1905
Colors Made: Crystal
Items/Values: Butter dish, 5¼" high, 7¼" across, $50.00. Cruet with original stopper (no stopper shown), $80.00. Celery vase, 6" high, 4⅝" across, $55.00.
Not Shown: Sugar with lid, $45.00. Creamer, $35.00. Spooner, $30.00.

Pattern: U.S. Regal, OMN: U.S. Glass No. 15098
Manufacturer: U.S. Glass Company, Glassport, Pennsylvania, factory "GP"
Date Introduced: c. 1906
Colors Made: Crystal, crystal w/rose blush
Items/Values: Butter dish, crystal w/rose blush and gold trim, 5¾" high, 8¼" across, $110.00. Sugar with lid, crystal w/rose blush and gold trim, 6³⁄₁₆" high, 6¾" across, $95.00. Creamer, crystal w/rose blush and gold trim, 3⅜" high, 5¾" across, $85.00. Spooner, crystal w/rose blush and gold trim, 3½" high, 3¾" across, $75.00.

Pattern: U.S. Sheraton
Manufacturer: U.S. Glass Company,
No. 15144
Date Introduced: c. 1912
Colors Made: Crystal, crystal
w/platinum, crystal w/rose blush
Items/Values: Butter dish, 5" high,
6½" across, $125.00. Sugar with
lid, 5½" high, 6½"across, $100.00.
Creamer, hotel, 2½" high, 5½"
across, $70.00. Spooner, 4⁷⁄₁₆"
high, 5⁷⁄₈" across, $55.00.
Not Shown: Creamer, regular, $80.00.
Notes: Values for plain crystal
pieces are 25% less than crystal
w/platinum. Values given are for
crystal w/platinum pieces.

Pattern: V In Heart
Manufacturer: Bryce, Higbee & Company, Pittsburgh, Pennsylvania
Date Introduced: c. 1895
Colors Made: Crystal
Items/Values: Creamer, 4⁵⁄₈" high, 4⁷⁄₈" across, $40.00.
Not Shown: Butter dish, $65.00. Sugar with lid, $50.00. Spooner, $35.00.

Pattern: Valencia Waffle, OMN: Adams' No. 85. AKA: Block and Star, Hexagonal Block
Manufacturer: Adams & Company, Pittsburgh, Pennsylvania, c. 1885; U.S. Glass Company,
Pittsburgh, Pennsylvania, after 1891
Date Introduced: c. 1885
Colors Made: Amber, apple green, blue, crystal, vaseline
Items/Values: Butter dish, crystal, 6⁵⁄₈" high, 5½" across, $65.00. Sugar with lid, crystal, 9⁵⁄₈"
high, 3⁷⁄₈" across, $60.00. Creamer, crystal, 5⁵⁄₈" high, 5⁷⁄₈" across, $50.00. Spooner, crystal,
5⁷⁄₈" high, 3⅜" across, $45.00.

Pattern: Vermont, OMN: U.S. Glass No. 15060 – Vermont. AKA: Honeycomb with Flower Rim, Inverted Thumbprint with Daisy Band, Vermont Honeycomb

Manufacturer: U.S. Glass Company, Pittsburgh, Pennsylvania, c. 1899 – 1903

Date Introduced: c. 1899

Colors Made: crystal, custard, emerald (plain or w/gold)

Reproductions: Toothpick by Boyd's Crystal Art Glass Company

Items/Values: Butter dish, crystal, 6⅛" high, 6¾" across, $110.00. Sugar with lid, crystal, 6⅛" high, 5⅛" across, $95.00. Creamer, crystal, 4¼" high, 6" across, $85.00. Spooner, crystal, 4⅛" high, 4¼" across, $70.00.

Pattern: Versailles

Manufacturer: Dithridge and Company, Pittsburgh, Pennsylvania

Date Introduced: c. 1900

Colors Made: Opaque w/decoration

Items/Values: Butter dish, 5¼" high, 7¼" across, $110.00. Sugar with lid, 6" high, 4⅜" across, $95.00. Creamer, 4⅞" high, 5⅛" across, $80.00. Spooner, 4⅜" high, 3¾" across, $85.00.

Pattern: Victoria, OMN: Fostoria No. 183

Manufacturer: Fostoria Glass Company, Fostoria, Ohio

Date Introduced: c. 1890

Colors Made: Crystal, crystal w/frost

Items/Values: Butter dish, crystal w/frost, 4½" high, 7¼" across, $295.00.

Not Shown: Sugar with lid, $250.00. Creamer, $150.00. Spooner, $125.00.

Notes: Values for plain crystal pieces are 20% less than crystal w/frost pieces. Values given are for crystal w/frost pieces.

Pattern: Viking, OMN: Hobbs' Centennial. AKA: Bearded Head, Bearded Prophet, Old Man of the Mountain(s)

Manufacturer: Hobbs, Brockunier & Company, Wheeling, West Virginia, designed by John H. Hobbs and patented under U.S. patent No. 9647 – November 21, 1876

Date Introduced: c. 1876

Colors Made: Crystal

Items/Values: Butter dish, 5¾" high, 6" across, $140.00. Sugar with lid, 7¾" high, 5¼" across, $115.00. Creamer, 4⅞" high, 6⅝" across, $95.00. Spooner, 4⅞" high, 3⅞" across, $80.00. Celery vase, 7" high, 4⅝" across, $100.00.

Pattern: Virginia, OMN: U.S. Glass No. 15071 – Virginia. AKA: Banded Portland Diamond, Banded Portland, Maiden's Blush, Portland with Diamond Point

Manufacturer: U.S. Glass Company, Pittsburgh, Pennsylvania, at factories "G," "U," and "E"

Date Introduced: c. 1901

Colors Made: Crystal, crystal w/blue, crystal w/green, crystal w/rose, crystal w/yellow

Items/Values: Butter dish, crystal, 5⅜" high, 8¼" across, $75.00.

Not Shown: Sugar with lid, $60.00. Creamer, $50.00. Spooner, $40.00.

Pattern: Waffle and Star Band, OMN: Verona. AKA: Block & Star Spear Point

Manufacturer: Tarentum Glass Company, Tarentum, Pennsylvania

Date Introduced: c. 1910

Colors Made: Crystal, crystal w/ruby stain

Items/Values: Butter dish, crystal, 4¾" high, 7⅝" across, $100.00. Sugar with lid, crystal, 6⅜" high, 4½" across, $75.00. Spooner, crystal, 4⅛" high, 3⅞" across, $50.00.

Not Shown: Creamer, $60.00.

Pattern: Washington (U.S. Glass), OMN: U.S. Glass No. 15074. AKA: Beaded Base, Late Washington
Manufacturer: U.S. Glass Company at factory "K" and factory "F," Pittsburgh, Pennsylvania
Date Introduced: c. 1901
Colors Made: Crystal, crystal w/decoration, crystal w/ruby stain (plain or w/gold)
Items/Values: Butter dish, crystal w/ decoration, 6" high, 7" across, $165.00. Sugar with lid, crystal w/decoration, 7³⁄₁₆" high, 4¼" across, $140.00. Creamer, crystal w/decoration, 5" high, 5" across, $85.00. Spooner, crystal w/decoration, 4¾" high, 3½" across, $75.00. Toothpick holder, crystal w/decoration, 2¾" high, 2¼" across, $60.00.

Pattern: Waverly
Manufacturer: Westmoreland Specialty Glass Company, Grapeville, Pennsylvania
Date Introduced: c. 1896
Colors Made: Crystal
Items/Values: Butter dish, 5½" high, 7¼" across, $70.00. Sugar with lid, no lid shown, 3¾" across, $65.00. Celery vase, 6⅛" high, 4⅛" across, $75.00.
Not Shown: Creamer, $50.00. Spooner, $45.00.

Pattern: Wedding Bells, OMN: Fostoria No. 789
Manufacturer: Fostoria Glass Company, Moundsville, West Virginia
Date Introduced: c. 1900
Colors Made: Crystal, crystal w/gold, maiden's blush, rose flash
Reproductions: Covered sugar (blot-purple)
Items/Values: Spooner, crystal w/gold, 4¼" high, 3⅞" across, $45.00
Not Shown: Butter dish, $75.00. Sugar with lid, $65.00. Creamer, $50.00.
Notes: Values for plain crystal pieces are 10% less than crystal w/gold. Values given are for crystal w/gold pieces.

Pattern: Westmoreland, OMN: Gillinder No. 420. AKA: Westmoreland Block
Manufacturer: Gillinder and Sons, U.S. Glass Company No. 15011, c. 1892
Date Introduced: c. 1888
Colors Made: Crystal
Items/Values: Butter dish, 5⅝" high, 7½" across, $80.00. Cruet, with original stopper, 6⅜" high, $100.00.
Not Shown: Sugar with lid, $70.00. Creamer, $55.00. Spooner, $45.00.

Pattern: Westmoreland's Priscilla, AKA: Divided Block with Sunburst
Manufacturer: Westmoreland Specialty Glass Company
Date Introduced: c. 1890s
Colors Made: Crystal
Items/Values: Butter dish, 5¾" high, 6¼" across, $75.00. Sugar with lid, 7¼" high, 3⅜" across, $60.00.
Not Shown: Creamer, $50.00. Spooner, $35.00.

Pattern: Westward Ho, OMN: Pioneer. AKA: Tippecanoe
Manufacturer: Gillinder & Sons, Philadelphia, Pennsylvania
Date Introduced: c. 1879
Colors Made: Crystal w/frost
Reproductions: Footed butter, celery vase, compotes, creamer, goblet, footed sherbet, footed sugar, tumbler, wine (crystal & frosted), by L.G. Wright Glass Company
Items/Values: Butter dish, 8⅞" high, 7¼" across, $425.00. Sugar with lid (no lid shown), 4½" across, $350.00. Creamer, 6¾" high, 6" across, $250.00.
Not Shown: Spooner, $195.00.

Pattern: Wheat and Barley, OMN: Duquesne. AKA: Hops and Barley, Oats and Barley
Manufacturer: Bryce Brothers, Pittsburgh, Pennsylvania, c. 1880s; U.S. Glass Company, Pittsburgh,Pennsylvania, at factory "B," after 1891
Date Introduced: c. 1880s
Colors Made: Amber, blue, canary, crystal
Reproductions: Goblet, crystal and in colors, by L.G. Wright Glass Company, unmarked

Items/Values: Butter dish, crystal, 5⅜" high, 7⅝" across, $75.00. Sugar with lid, crystal, 7¾" high, 4¼" across, $80.00. Creamer, crystal, 5" high, 5" across, $65.00. Spooner, crystal, 4⅜" high, 3⅜" across, $60.00.

Pattern: Willow Oak, OMN: Bryce's Wreath. AKA: Acorn, Acorn and Oak Leaf, Oak Leaf, Stippled Daisy, Thistle and Sunflower, Willow and Oak

Manufacturer: Bryce Brothers, Pittsburgh, Pennsylvania, U.S. Glass Company at factory "B," c. 1891

Date Introduced: c. 1880

Colors Made: Amber, blue, canary yellow, crystal

Items/Values: Butter dish, crystal, 5½" high, 7 5/16" across, $50.00.

Not Shown: Sugar with lid, $45.00. Creamer, $35.00. Spooner, $30.00.

Pattern: Wiltec

Manufacturer: McKee Glass Company, Jeannette, Pennsylvania

Date Introduced: c. 1904

Colors Made: Crystal

Items/Values: Butter dish, 5½" high, 8" across, $85.00. Sugar with lid, 5¾" high, 7⅜" across, $75.00. Creamer, 3⅜" high, 6" across, $50.00.

Not Shown: Spooner, $45.00.

Notes: One of the well-advertised "Tec" patterns. Pieces are usually marked with McKee's "Prescut" mark.

Pattern: Winged Scroll, OMN: No. 1280
Manufacturer: A.H. Heisey Glass Company, Newark, Ohio, c. 1899 – 1901
Date Introduced: c. 1899
Colors Made: Custard w/gold, emerald w/gold (see Notes)
Items/Values: Butter dish, custard w/gold, 4¹³⁄₁₆" high, 7½" across, $175.00.
Not Shown: Sugar with lid, custard, $150.00. Creamer, custard, $100.00. Spooner, custard, $105.00, Toothpick holder, custard, $250.00.
Notes: Colors of crystal, canary, and opal are scarce.

Pattern: Winged Scroll, OMN: No. 1280
Manufacturer: A.H. Heisey Glass Company, Newark, Ohio, c. 1899 – 1901
Date Introduced: c. 1899
Colors Made: Custard w/gold, emerald w/gold (see Notes)
Items/Values: Butter dish, emerald w/gold, 4¾" high, 7½" across, $175.00.
Not Shown: Sugar with lid, emerald w/gold, $150.00. Creamer, emerald w/gold, $100.00. Spooner, emerald w/gold, $105.00. Toothpick holder, emerald w/gold, $250.00.
Notes: Colors of crystal, canary, and opal are scarce.

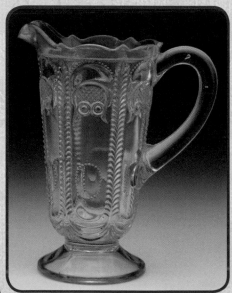

Pattern: Wyoming, OMN: U.S. Glass No. 15081 – Wyoming. AKA: Enigma, Bull's Eye
Manufacturer: U.S. Glass Company, Pittsburgh, Pennsylvania, at factory "U" and factory "E"
Date Introduced: c. 1903
Colors Made: Crystal
Items/Values: Creamer, individual, open, 4⅞" high, 2⅝" across, $35.00.
Not Shown: Butter dish, $275.00. Sugar with lid, $180.00. Creamer, individual, covered, $100.00. Creamer, table, $95.00. Spooner, $110.00.

Pattern: X-Ray
Manufacturer: Riverside Glass Works, Wellsburg, West Virginia
Date Introduced: c. 1896
Colors Made: Amethyst, crystal, crystal w/gold, emerald green
Items/Values: Butter dish, 5¼" high, 7½" across, $70.00.
Not Shown: Sugar with lid, $55.00. Creamer, $45.00. Spooner, $40.00.
Notes: Values for plain crystal pieces are 10% less than crystal w/gold. Values given are for crystal w/gold pieces.

Pattern: Yale, AKA: Crow Feet
Manufacturer: McKee & Brothers, Pittsburgh, Pennsylvania
Date Introduced: c. 1880s
Colors Made: Crystal
Items/Values: Butter dish, 5⅝" high, 7¼" across, $95.00. Sugar with lid, 7⅞" high, 4¼" across, $80.00. Creamer, 5½" high, 4⅝" across, $65.00. Spooner, 5³⁄₁₆" high, 3¼" across, $75.00.

Pattern: Yutec
Manufacturer: McKee & Brothers
Date Introduced: c. 1909
Colors Made: Crystal
Reproductions: Some in colors by Mosser? L.E. Smith? Kemple?
Items/Values: Cruet with original stopper (no stopper shown), $45.00.
Not Shown: Butter dish, $50.00. Sugar with lid, $40.00. Creamer, $30.00. Spooner, $25.00.

Pattern: Zipper Cross, OMN: Paris. AKA: Roughneck,
New Martinsville No. 110
Manufacturer: Bryce, Higbee & Company, 1899 - 1907;
J.B. Higbee Glass Company, c. 1907; New Martinsville
Glass Manufacturing Company, c. 1919
Date Introduced: c. 1899
Colors Made: Crystal
Items/Values: Butter dish, 5⅝" high, 8⅛" across, $60.00.
Not Shown: Sugar with lid, $50.00. Creamer, $40.00.
Spooner, $25.00.

Pattern: Zipper Slash, OMN: No. 2500
Manufacturer: George Duncan's Sons and
Company, Washington, Pennsylvania
Date Introduced: c. 1893
Colors Made: Crystal, crystal w/amber
stain, crystal w/etch, crystal w/frost,
crystal w/ruby stain
Items/Values: Sugar with lid, 7" high, 3⅞"
across, $60.00. Creamer, 5¾" high, 4¾"
across, $50.00. Spooner, 4¼" high, 3¼"
across, $40.00.
Not Shown: Butter dish, $75.00.
Notes: Values for plain crystal pieces are
10% less than crystal w/etch. Values
given are for crystal w/etch pieces.

Pattern: Zippered Heart, OMN:
No. 292
Manufacturer: Imperial Glass
Company, Bellaire, Ohio
Date Introduced: c. 1912
Colors Made: Crystal
Items/Values: Sugar, individual,
square, 3⅞" high, 6¾" across,
$35.00. Creamer, 4¾" high,
5⅜" across, $65.00. Spoon
tray, double handle, 3⅝" high,
5⅞" long, $65.00.
Not Shown: Butter dish,
$115.00. Sugar with lid
(regular), $95.00. Spooner,
$55.00.

Bibliography

Archer, Margaret & Douglas. *Imperial Glass Company 1904 – 1938 catalogs 104F, 101D, Bargain Book, Cat. B.* 1978, values updated 1993.

Batty, Bob H. *A Complete Guide to Pressed Glass.* Gretna, LA: Pelican Publishing Company, 1978.

Bond, Marcelle. *The Beauty of Albany Glass, 1893 to 1902.* Berne, IN: Publishers Printing House, Marcelle Bond, 1972.

Bones, Frances. *The Book of Duncan Glass.* Des Moines, IA: Wallace-Homestead Book Company, 1973.

Bredehoft, Neila & Tom. *Heisey Glass: 1896 – 1957, Identification & Value Guide,* Paducah, KY: Collector Books, 2001. Values updated 2003.

Bredehoft, Tom. *Glass Tumblers, 1860s to 1920s.* Paducah, KY: Collector Books, 2004.

The Cambridge Glass Company *1903 Catalog of Pressed & Blown Glassware.* Cambridge, OH: Southeastern Printing Company, 1976.

Chervenka, Mark J. *The Black Light Book for Antiques & Collectibles, Updated 4th Edition.* Antique & Collector's Reproduction News, Mark J. Chervenka, 1998.

Computer Info Newsletter (Square Adams & Company, Pittsburgh, PA c. 1882 – 1887) *The Glass Club Bulletin,* #163, Winter/Fall, 1990/1991, reprinted 2-2-2001.

Co-Operative Flint Glass Company catalog, Beaver Falls, PA.

Dunbar, Shirley. *Heisey Glass, The Early Years: 1896 – 1924.* Iola, WI: Krause Publications, 2000.

Early American Pattern Glass Society. *News Journal,* Vol. 10, #3, Fall 2003.

Edwards, Bill and Mike Carwile. *Standard Encyclopedia of Millersburg Crystal, Identification and Values.* Paducah, KY: Collector Books, 2001.

___. *Standard Encyclopedia of Opalescent Glassware, Fifth Edition.* Paducah, KY: Collector Books, 2005.

___. *Standard Encyclopedia of Opalescent Glassware, Fourth Edition.* Paducah, KY: Collector Books, 2002.

___. *Standard Encyclopedia of Pressed Glass, 1860 – 1930, Identification & Values.* Paducah, KY: Collector Books, 1999.

___. *Standard Encyclopedia of Pressed Glass, Second Edition, 1860 – 1930, Identification & Values.* Paducah, KY: Collector Books, 2000.

___. *Standard Encyclopedia of Pressed Glass, Third Edition, 1860 – 1930, Identification & Values.* Paducah, KY: Collector Books, 2003.

___. *Standard Encyclopedia of Pressed Glass, Fourth Edition, 1860 – 1930, Identification & Values.* Paducah, KY: Collector Books, 2005.

Ezell, Elaine & George Newhouse. *Cruets Cruets; Cruets, Volume II.* Marietta, OH: Antique Publications, 1993.

Florence, Gene and Cathy. *Elegant Glassware of the Depression Era, 11th Edition.* Paducah, KY: Collector Books, 2005.

___. *Florences' Glassware Pattern Identification Guide, Volume I.* Paducah, KY: Collector Books, 1998.

___. *Florences' Glassware Pattern Identification Guide, Volume II.* Paducah, KY: Collector Books, 2000.

___. *Florences' Glassware Pattern Identification Guide, Volume III.* Paducah, KY: Collector Books, 2003.

___. *Florences' Glassware Pattern Identification Guide, Volume IV.* Paducah, KY: Collector Books, 2005.

Gorham, C.W. *Riverside Glass Works of Wellsburg, West Virginia, 1879 – 1907.* C.W. Gorham, 1995.

Hallock, Marilyn R. *Central Glass Company, The First 30 Years, 1863 – 1893.* Atglen, PA: Schiffer Publishing, Ltd., 2002.

Hartley, Julia Magee & Mary Magee Cobb. *The States' Series Early American Pattern Glass.* Julia Magee Hartley and Mary Magee Cobb, 1976.

Heacock, William. *Collecting Glass Volume I.* Marietta, OH: Antique Publications, 1984.

___. *Collecting Glass, Volume 2.* Marietta, OH: Antique Publications, 1985.

___. *Collecting Glass, Volume 3.* Marietta, OH: Antique Publications, 1986.

___. *Encyclopedia of Victorian Colored Pattern Glass, Book I, Toothpick Holders from A to Z.* Marietta, OH: Richardson Printing Corp., 1976.

___. *Encyclopedia of Victorian Colored Pattern Glass, Book II, Opalescent Glass from A to Z, Ed. 2.* Marietta, OH: Richardson Printing Corp., 1975.

___. *Encyclopedia of Victorian Colored Pattern Glass, Book III, Syrups, Sugar Shakers, & Cruets from A to Z.* Marietta, OH: Richardson Printing Corporation, 1976.

___. *Encyclopedia of Victorian Colored Pattern Glass, Book 4, Custard Glass from A to Z.* Marietta, OH: Richardson Printing Corp., 1976.

___. *Encyclopedia of Victorian Colored Pattern Glass, Book 5, US Glass from A to Z.* Marietta, OH: Richardson Printing Corp., 1978.

___. *Encyclopedia of Victorian Colored Pattern Glass, Book 6, Oil Cruets from A to Z.* Marietta, OH: Richardson Printing Corp., 1981.

___. *Encyclopedia of Victorian Colored Pattern Glass, Book 7, Ruby Stained from A to Z.* Marietta, OH: Antique Publications, Inc., 1986.

___. *The Glass Collector Issue Number Five.* Columbus, OH: Peacock Publications, Winter 1983.

___. *The Glass Collector Issue Number Four.* Columbus, OH: Peacock Publications, Fall 1982.

___. *The Glass Collector Issue Number Six.* Columbus, OH: Peacock Publications, Summer 1983.

___. *The Glass Collector Issue Number Three.* Columbus, OH: Peacock Publications, Summer 1982.

___. *The Glass Collector Issue Number Two.* Columbus, OH: Peacock Publications, Spring 1982.

___. *The Glass Collector Premiere Issue.* Columbus, OH: Peacock Publications, Winter 1982.

___. *Old Pattern Glass According to Heacock.* Marietta, OH: Antique Publications, 1981.

Heacock, William and Fred Bickenheuser. *Encyclopedia of Victorian Colored Pattern Glass, Book 5, U.S. Glass from A to Z.* Marietta, OH: Richardson Printing Corp., 1978.

Heacock, William, James Measell, and Berry Wiggins. *Harry Northwood, The Early Years, 1881 – 1900.* Marietta, OH: Antique Publications, 1990.

____. *Harry Northwood, The Wheeling Years, 1901 – 1925.* Marietta, OH: Antique Publications, 1991.

Hicks, Joyce A. *Just Jenkins.* 1988.

Higby, Lola & Wayne. *Bryce, Higbee & J.B. Higbee Glass.* Marietta, OH: The Glass Press, Inc. dba Antique Publications.

Husfloen, Kyle. *Collector's Guide to American Pressed Glass 1825 – 1915.* Kyle D. Husfloen, 1992.

Innes, Lowell. *Pittsburgh Glass, 1797 – 1891.* Lowell Innes, 1976.

Jenks, Bill, Jerry Luna, and Darryl Reilly. *Identifying Pattern Glass Reproductions.* Radnor, PA: Wallace-Homestead Book Company, 1993.

Kamm, Minnie Watson. *A First Two Hundred Pattern Glass Pitcher.* Grosse Point, MI: Kamm Publications, 1970.

___. *A Second Two Hundred Pattern Glass Pitcher.* Grosse Point, MI: Kamm Publications, 1950.

___. *A Third Two Hundred Pattern Glass Pitcher.* Grosse Point, MI: Kamm Publications, 1953.

___. *A Fourth Two Hundred Pattern Glass Pitcher.* Grosse Point, MI: Kamm Publications, 1950.

___. *A Fifth Pattern Glass Book.* Grosse Point, MI: Kamm Publications, 1970.

___. *A Sixth Pattern Glass Book.* Grosse Point. MI: Kamm Publications, 1970.

___. *A Seventh Pattern Glass Book.* Grosse Point. MI: Kamm Publications, 1970.

___. *An Eighth Pattern Glass Book.* Grosse Point, MI: Kamm Publications, 1970.

Kamm-Wood. *Encyclopedia of Antique Pattern Glass, Vols. I and II.* Watkins Glen, NY: Century House, 1961.

Krause, Gail. *The Encyclopedia of Duncan Glass,* 1976.

___. *The Years of Duncan, 1865 – 1955, Patterns Spanning the Ninety Years of Producing "The Loveliest Glassware in America."* Heyworth, IL: Heyworth Star, 1980.

Lee, Ruth Webb. *Early American Pressed Glass.* Wellesley Hills 81, MA: Lee Publications, by Robert W. Lee, 1960.

___. *Ruth Webb Lee's Handbook of Early American Pressed Glass Patterns.* Rutland, VT and Tokyo, Japan: Charles E. Tuttle Company, Inc., 1984.

___. *Ruth Webb Lee's Victorian Glass Handbook.* Rutland, VT and Tokyo, Japan: Charles E. Tuttle Company, Inc., 1984.

Lucas, Robert Irwin. *Tarentum Pattern Glass.* Tarentum, PA: Buhl Bros. Printing, 1981.

McCain, Mollie Helen. *The Collector's Encyclopedia of Pattern Glass.* Paducah, KY: Collector Books, 1982. Values updated 1998.

___. *Field Guide to Pattern Glass.* Paducah, KY: Collector Books, 2000.

Measell, James. *Greentown Glass, the Indiana Tumbler & Goblet Company.* Grand Rapids, MI: The Grand Rapids Public Museum, 1979.

___. *New Martinsville Glass, 1900 – 1944.* Marietta, OH: Antique Publications, 1994.

Measell, James and Don E. Smith. *Findlay Glass, The Glass Tableware Manufacturers, 1886 – 1902.* Marietta, OH: Antique Publications, Inc., 1986.

Metz, Alice Hulett. *Early American Pattern Glass.* Paducah, KY: Collector Books, 2000.

___. *Much More Early American Pattern Glass.* Paducah, KY: Collector Books, 2000.

Miles, Dori & Robert W. Miller. *Wallace-Homestead Price Guide to Pattern Glass, Eleventh Edition.* Radnor, PA: Wallace-Homestead, 1986.

Millard, S.T. *Goblets II.* Holton, KS: Gosspi. Printers and Publishers, 1940.

Miller, Everett & Addie. *The New Martinsville Glass Story, New Martinsville Glass Mfg. Company, NM, WV.* Marietta, OH: Richardson Publishing Company, 1972.

Miller, Robert W. *Wallace-Homestead Price Guide to Antiques & Pattern Glass, Fourth Edition.* Des Moines, IA: Wallace-Homestead Book Company, 1977.

___. *Wallace-Homestead Price Guide to Antiques & Pattern Glass, Sixth Edition.* Des Moines, IA: Wallace-Homestead, 1979.

Mordock, John B. & Walter L. Adams. *Pattern Glass Mugs.* Marietta, OH: The Glass Press, Inc., 1995.

Peterson, Arthur G. *Glass Patents and Patterns.* Sanford, FL: Celery City Printing Company, 1973.

Pina, Leslie. *Fostoria Serving The American Table 1887 – 1986.* Atglen, PA: Schiffer Publishing, Ltd., 2002.

Reilly, Darryl and Bill Jenks. *Early American Pattern Glass, 2nd Edition, Collector's Identification & Pattern Guide,* Iola, WI: Krause Publications, 2002.

___. *U.S. Glass, The States Patterns, An Identification and Value Guide.* West Wyoming, PA: Jones Offset Printing, 1998.

Revi, Albert Christen. *American Pressed Glass and Figural Bottles.* Nashville, NY: Thomas Nelson, Inc., 1972.

Sanford, Jo & Bob. *The Canton Glass Company of Canton, Ohio, 1883 – 1890.* Marion, IN, 1890 – 1899. Researched Glass Facts, 1998.

Schroy, Ellen Tischbein. *Warman's Pattern Glass.* Radnor, PA: Rinker Enterprises, Inc., 1993.

Spillman, Jane Shadel. "Adams and Company, A Closer Look." *EAPG Newsletter,* The Glass Club Bulletin, 1990 – 1991.

Stout, Sandra McPhee. *The Complete McKee Glass.* North Kansas City, MO: The Trojan Press, 1972.

Teal, Ron, Sr., edited by Tarez Samragraban. *Albany Glass Model Flint Glass Company of Albany, IN.* Marietta, OH: The Glass Press, Inc., dba Antique Publications, 1997.

Unitt, Doris & Peter. *American & Canadian Goblets.* Petersborough, Ontario, Canada: Clock House, 1970. Reissued 1975, For the Love of Glass Publishing, Inc.

___. *American & Canadian Goblets, Vol. II.* Wilbur, Ontario, Canada: For the Love of Glass Publishing, Inc., 1994. Reissued 1994, For the Love of Glass Publishing, Inc.

Weatherman, Hazel Marie. *Fostoria, The First Fifty Years.* Springfield, MO: The Weathermans, 1972.

Welker, John & Elizabeth. *Pressed Glass in America — Encyclopedia of The First Hundred Years; 1825 – 1925.* Ivyland, PA: Antique Acres Press, 1985.

Wilson, Charles West. *Westmoreland Glass, Identification & Value Guide.* Paducah, KY: Collector Books, 1996.

Index

1-0-1 128
153 Pattern 151
327 Pattern 117
1205 68
1205½ 68
1255 89
Acanthus Leaf 75
Acorn 183
Acorn and Oak Leaf 183
Actress 6
Ada 6
Adam's, Bellaire No. 456 48
Adams' No. 3 140
Adams' No. 5 91
Adams' No. 85 177
Adams' No. 130 6
Adams' Thousand Eye 6
Admiral 148
Adonis 7
Aegis 7
Aida 8
Akron Block 149
Alabama 8
Alaska 8
Albany 10, 24
Albion 9
Alexis 9, 53
Amazon 10
Amberette 105
American Beauty 55

American Bow Tie 29
Amulet 125
Annie 6
Anona 176
Anthemion 10
Apollo 11
Archaic Gothic 20
Arched Cane & Fan 35
Arched Diamond Points 119
Arched Fleur-de-Lis 11
Arched Ovals 12
Arrowhead 139
Art 12
Ashman 12
Athenia 146
Atlanta 13
Atlas 14
Atlas (Northwood) 13
Avon 14
Aztec 14
Baby Thumbprint 52
Bagware 87
Bakewell Ribbon 15
Balder 137
Baltimore Pear 15
Bamboo 16
Bamboo Edge 16
Banded Portland 179
Banded Portland Diamond 179
Banded Stalks 155

Banded Star 16
Banded Thousand Eye 6
Banner 16
Barberry 17
Barley 17
Barred Star 164
Barreled Block 145
Bars and Buttons 149
Batesville 18
Bead & Bar Medallion 7
Bead and Scroll 18
Bead Column 18
Beaded Acorn 19
Beaded Arch 20
Beaded Arch Panels 20
Beaded Base 180
Beaded Bull's Eye and Drape 8
Beaded Dart Band 20
Beaded Diamond Band 20
Beaded Grape 33
Beaded Grape and Vine 33
Beaded Grape Medallion 20
Beaded Loop(s) 129
Beaded Man 143
Beaded Medallion 21
Beaded Mirror 21
Beaded 101 128
Beaded Oval & Scroll 21
Beaded Ovals 129
Beaded Panel & Sunburst 22

Beaded Swirl 22
Beaded Swirl and Disc 22
Beaded Triangle 59
Bead Swag 19
Bean 62
Bearded Head 179
Bearded Prophet 179
Bellaire No. 456 48
Belmont No. 100 23
Belt Buckle 102
Bent Buckle 124
Berry 17
Bethlehem Star 23
Beveled Diamond & Star 24
Big Button 26
Bird and Strawberry 24
Bird in Ring 102
Blazing Cornucopia 24
Blazing Pinwheels 156
Bleeding Heart 25
Block and Fan 26
Block and Circle 25
Block and Lattice 26
Block and Pleat 27
Block and Star 26, 177
Block & Star Spear Point 179
Block Barrel 84
Blockhouse 85
Block with Stars 85
Blooms and Blossoms 121

Blue Bird	24	Chain	38
Blue Jay	36	Chain with Star	38
Blue Thumbprint	105	Champion	39
Bordered Ellipse	27	Chandelier	39
Bosc Pear	28	Cherry and Gable	40
Bosworth	163	Cherry Thumbprint	40
Bow Tie	29	Chesterfield	40
Brazil	131	Chick	76
Bright Star	23	Chicken	76
Brilliant	131	Chickenwire	152
Britannic	29	Chimo	128
Bryce	148	Church Windows	40
Bryce Double Loop	148	Clarissa	93
Bryce Fashion	29	Classic	41
Bryce No. 1 – Tulip	176	Classic Medallion	41
Bryce No. 79	38	Clear Block	145
Bryce No. 175	38, 145	Clear Diagonal Band	42
Bryce's Royal	162	Clear Lion Head	75
Bryce's Wreath	183	Clematis	151
Buckle	30	Clio	42
Buckle and Star	30	Coarse Zig-Zag	43
Buckle with Star	30	Colonial	44
Bullet	14, 32	Colonial & Mitre	76
Bullet Emblem	32	Colonis	44
Bull's Eye	139, 184	Colorado	45
Bull's Eye and Daisy	31	Columbia	40, 87
Bull's Eye & Diamond Point	147	Columbian	87
Bull's Eye and Fan	31	Columbia with Pie Crust Edge	46
Bull's Eye and Star	122	Comet	33
Bull's Eye Band	147	Comet in the Stars	46
Bull's Eye in Heart	87	Compact	159
Bull's Eye with Diamond Point	147	Concave Block	13
Butterfly and Fan	102	Concaved Almond	12
Button and Buckle	172	Connecticut	46
Button Arches	32	Co-Op No. 276	43
Button Panel	33	Coral	71
Buzz Star	33	Cord Drapery	47
Caldonia	36	Corner Medallion	47
California	33	Corrigan	48
California State	42	Cosmos	48
Cambridge Buzz Saw	35	Cottage	48
Cambridge Feather	68	Cradled Diamonds	53
Cambridge Glass No. 669	68	Creased Hexagon Block	90
Cambridge No. 2504	34	Crescent No. 601	58
Cambridge No. 2692	34	Cromwell	106
Cambridge No. 2760	34	Cross Roads	12
Cambridge No. 2870 – Strawberry	99	Crossed Discs (Disks)	49
Cameo	41	Crossed Ovals	49
Canadian Drape	79	Crow Feet	185
Canadian Horseshoe	11	Crown and Shield	49
Canadian Thistle	132	Crystal Ball	14, 67
Cane Horseshoe	35	Crystal Circle	77
Cane Insert	35	Cube with Fan	138
Cane Variant	119	Cupid and Venus	50
Cannon Ball	14, 67	Curtain Tie Back	50
Cannonball Pinwheel	36	Cut Log	50
Canton No. 10	143	Dahlia	51
Captain Kid – 150	145	Dahlia with/and Petals	60
Cardinal	36	Daisies in Oval Panels	31
Cardinal Bird	36	Daisy	107
Carmen	37	Daisy & Button Panelled	132
Carolina	37	Daisy and Button Petticoat	165
Cathedral	37	Daisy and Button Plain	23
Cat's Eye and Block	50	Daisy and Button Scalloped Edge	23
Celtic	38	Daisy and Button - Single Panel	132
Central's No. 881	145	Daisy and Button with Clear Lily	51
Central's No. 893	145	Daisy and Button with Narcissus	51
Daisy and Button with Oval Panels	85	Doyle No. 25	82
Daisy and Button with Petticoat Band	165	Doyle No. 76	175
Daisy and Panel	131	Doyle No. 250	145
Daisy Band	165	Drum	146
Daisy Button & Almond Band	42	Duncan & Miller No. 52	108
Daisy Drape	52	Duncan & Miller No. 73	173
Daisy with X Band	78	Duncan No. 20	83
Dakota	52	Duncan No. 39	32
Dalton	53	Duncan No. 42	116
Dalzell No. 75	105	Duncan No. 128 – Arizona	170
Dalzell No. 75D	105	Duncan No. 555	156
Dalzell No. 490D	147	Duncan No. 600	20
Dalzell's Priscilla	53	Duncan No. 800	87
Dart	54	Duncan's No. 30	152
Deer & Doe	54	Duncan's No. 72	61
Deer and Pine Tree	54	Duncan's No. 150	77
Delaware	55	Duncan's No. 328	145
Delta	132	Duncan's No. 360 Ware	159
Derby	140	Duquesne	182
Dewdrop and Rain	55	Eagle and Arms	32
Dewdrop and Raindrop	55	Eagle and Shield	32
Dewdrop and Star	56	Earl	161
Dewdrop with Small Star	56	Early	30
Dewdrop with Star	56	Early Oregon	158
Dewey	56	Effulgent Star	61
Dew with Raindrop	55	Egg in Sand	62
Diagonal Band with Fan	56	Egyptian	62
Diamond and Long Sunburst	39	Electric	63
Diamond and Teardop	169	Elephant Toes	63
Diamond Bar	108	Elite	138
Diamond Beaded Band	120	Ellrose	132
Diamond Block with Fan	57	Elmino	157
Diamond Bridges	57	Emblem	32
Diamond Crystal	33	Emerald Green Herringbone	72
Diamond Flute	57	Empire	90, 116
Diamond Gold	74	Empress	64
Diamond Lattice	40	English Hobnail Cross	105
Diamond Medallion	81	English Hobnail Variant	168
Diamond Point Discs	58	Engraving No. 189	157
Diamond Point Disk	58	Enigma	184
Diamond Point Loop	58	Era	64
Diamond Prisms	24	Estelle	44
Diamond Pyramids	59	Esther	65
Diamonds and Bull's Eye Band	147	Esther Ware	65
Diamond's No. 206 – New Century	55	Etched Fern and Waffle	118
Diamonds with Double Fans	59	Ethol	50
Diamond Waffle	59	Eureka	66
Diamond with Double Fans	155	Eva	145
Dinner Bell	48	Evangeline	66
Divided Block with Sunburst	181	Excelsior	105
Divided Medallion with Diamond Cut	152	Eyewinker	67
Divided Squares	92	Fagot	67
Dolphin	60	Famous	136
Dolphin Stem	60	Fancy Diamonds	173
Dominion	118	Fancy Loop	67
Dot	21, 166	Fandango	68
Double Arch	64	Fan with Crossbars	39
Double Dahlia with Lens	60	Fan with Diamond	68
Double Fan	60	Feather	68
Double Loop	148, 166	Feather and Quill	68
Double Pear	15	Feather Band	69
Double Pinwheel	61	Feather Duster	69
Double Red Block	90	Feathered Swirl	160
Double Snail	159	Federal No. 50	55
		Ferris Wheel	70
		Festoon	70
		Festoons and Sunbursts	163
		Field Thistle	71
		Figure Eight	148

Fine Cut & Diamond 81
Fine Cut and Feather................ 68
Fine Cut and Ribbed Bars........ 108
Fine Cut Band 48, 71
Fine Cut Bar 130
Fine Cut Medallion 81
Fisheye................................ 174
Fish Scale 71
Flamboyant............................ 57
Flaming Thistle 71
Flat to Round Panel 173
Fleur-de-Lis and Drape 72
Fleur-de-Lis and Tassel 72
Fleur-de-Lis Scrolled 100
Floral Diamond 156
Floral Panel......................... 150
Florida.................................. 72
Florida Palm 174
Flower and Bud 121
Flower and Diamond 73
Flower and Honeycomb 73
Flower Fan 159
Flower Flange 56
Flower Plant.......................... 73
Flower Pot............................. 73
Flower Spray with Scrolls........ 98
Flower with Cane 74
Flying Bird and Strawberry....... 24
Forest 101
Forest Ware 101
Forget-Me-Not in Snow.......... 166
Fort Pitt................................ 74
Fostoria 74
Fostoria No. 140 145
Fostoria No. 183 178
Fostoria No. 500 – Atlanta........ 75
Fostoria No. 576 49
Fostoria No. 603 150
Fostoria No. 789 180
Fostoria No. 1630.................... 9
Fostoria No. 1121 113
Fostoria's Atlanta.................... 75
Fostoria's No. 676 75
Fostoria's Priscilla 75
Four Petal Flower 55
Frisco 75
Frontier 76
Frosted Amberette................. 105
Frosted Atlanta 75
Frosted Chain......................... 38
Frosted Chicken 76
Frosted Circle 77
Frosted Eagle 77
Frosted Festal Ball.................. 11
Frosted Hawk......................... 77
Frosted Lion 111
Frosted Ribbon.................. 15, 77
Frosted Waffle 91
Gala 78
Galloway................................ 78
Garfield Drape 79
Gem 79, 163
Geneva 80, 119
George Duncan No. 335.......... 22
Georgia................................. 80
Georgia Gem 80
Gibson Girl 81
Gillinder No. 15...................... 30
Gillinder No. 414................... 164

Gillinder No. 420................... 181
Gillinder's Centennial............. 109
Good Luck............................. 81
Grace.................................. 102
Granby................................ 113
Grand................................... 81
Grape and Cable 82
Grape and Festoon 82
Grape and Vine...................... 33
Grape with Vine...................... 82
Grasshopper.......................... 83
Grated Diamond & Sunburst........83
Greek................................... 56
Greensburg's No. 130............. 84
Greentown No. 11 39
Grenade................................ 84
Grille.................................... 85
Guardian Angel...................... 50
Guernsey Near Cut................. 34
Gypsy 15
Hand.................................. 137
Hanover................................ 85
Hanover Star......................... 85
Hartley.................................. 85
Harvard Yard..................... 4, 86
Hawaiian Lei.......................... 78
Heart and Thumbprint 87
Heart Plume........................ 117
Hearts and Spades................ 120
Heart Stem 86
Heart with Thumbprint............. 87
Heavy Drape.......................... 87
Heavy Finecut........................ 87
Heavy Gothic......................... 88
Heavy Panelled Finecut........... 88
Hedlin Shell 156
Heisey's Pineapple & Fan........ 89
Hero.................................... 89
Herringbone Band 90
Hexagonal Block 177
Hexagonal Bull's Eye.............. 90
Hickman 90
Hidalgo................................. 91
High Hob............................... 91
Highland................................ 43
Hobbs' Block......................... 92
Hobbs' Centennial................ 179
Hobbs' No. 330...................... 92
Hobbs' No. 339..................... 108
Hobnail Pointed (Ball Feet)....... 92
Holbrook.............................. 138
Honeycomb with Flower Rim.... 178
Hops and Barley 182
Horsemint.............................. 95
Horseshoe............................. 81
Horseshoe Daisy 93
Huckle 69
Idaho.................................. 159
IHC.................................... 171
Illinois.................................. 93
Imperial............................... 103
Imperial No. 1 173
Indiana.................................. 93
Indiana Feather...................... 94
Indiana Glass No. 124 51
Indiana Glass No. 157 24
Indiana's Colonial 95
Indiana's Elite No. 123............ 96
Indiana Sensation................... 94

"Indiana Silver"....................... 94
Indiana's No. 127................... 135
Indiana's No. 156................... 97
Indiana Swirl 68
Indiana Tumbler No. 350 47
Indian Tree 162
Intaglio................................. 98
Intaglio Sunflower................... 98
Interlocked Hearts 99
Inverness 37
Inverted Imperial.................... 59
Inverted Loop(s) and Fan(s).... 118
Inverted Prism...................... 118
Inverted Strawberry................ 99
Inverted Thistle...................... 99
Inverted Thumbprint with Daisy
   Band 178
Iowa 100
Iris.................................... 100
Iris with Meander 100
Ivanhoe.............................. 101
Ivy in Snow......................... 101
Ivy in Snow – Red Leaves 101
Jacob's Tears........................ 12
Japanese............................ 101
Japanese Fan...................... 102
Japanese Iris....................... 102
Jasper................................. 102
Jefferson's No. 15061 78
Jenny Lind 6
Jewel................................... 45
Jewel and Crescent............... 170
Jewel & Dewdrop 104
Jewel and Festoon 111
Jeweled Diamond and Fan....... 168
Jeweled Moon and Star 157
Jeweled Moon & Stars 103
Jeweled Rose(s) 170
Jewel with Dewdrop 104
Jewel with Dewdrops 104
Jewel with Moon and Star....... 157
Job's Tears 12
Josephine's Fan 34
Jubilee No. 1 90
Jumbo 103
Jungle 71
Juno.................................... 61
Kamoni 137
Kansas............................... 104
Kentucky 104
King's Crown 105
King's Floral Ware.................. 25
Klear-Kut No. 705................. 105
Klondike.............................. 105
Klondyke............................. 105
Knobby Bottom 14
Knobby Bull's Eye 31, 106
Kokomo-Jenkins No. 514........ 171
Kokomo No. 8 104
Kokomo No. 50 55
LaBelle No. 365 16
La Belle Rose 107
La Clede 90
Lacy Daisy 107
Lacy Jewel............................ 45
Lacy Medallion....................... 45
Ladders 107
Ladders and Diamonds with
   Star................................. 130

Ladders with Diamonds 108
Late Buckle........................... 102
Late Buckle and Star.............. 30
Late Lion............................... 75
Late Moon and Star.......... 53, 103
Late Sawtooth 150
Late Strawberry Variant........... 99
Late Thistle........................... 99
Late Washington.................. 180
Lattice................................ 108
Leaf and Flower.................... 108
Leaf and Star....................... 109
Legged Banded Star 16
Liberty Bell.......................... 109
Lily of the Valley................... 110
Lily of the Valley on Legs....... 110
Lion.................................... 111
Lion and Cable 110
Lion's Leg 8
Little Gem 80
Little Shrine 157
Locket................................ 126
Locust.................................. 83
Lone Star 163
Long Diamond 141
Long Leaf Teasel 111
Long Spear............................ 83
Long Star 171
Loop and Diamond 118
Loop and Jewel 111
Loop & Pillar 121
Loop and Pyramid(s) 107
Loops and Drops 124
Loop(s) and Fan(s)................ 118
Loop with Dewdrop 112
Loop with Pillar.................... 121
Loop with Stippled Panels 171
Lorne 112
Louise 113
Louisiana 113
Louis XV 112
Lucile 70
Madeira 114
Maiden's Blush.............. 124, 179
Maine 114
Manhattan 115
Mardi Gras.......................... 116
Mardi Gras with Thumbprints . 115
Marlboro 117
Marsh Fern 117
Maryland............................. 118
Maryland Pear 15
Mascotte 118
Masonic 118
Massachusetts 119
Mayflower...................... 37, 110
McKee No. 3 – Shell 67
McKee's Band Diamond.......... 54
McKee's Comet 119
McKee's Doric 68
McKee's Gothic 119
McKee's No. 79 27
McKee's Stars & Stripes........ 120
Medallion...................... 81, 120
Mellor 26
Melrose 120
Michigan 121
Midway 121, 138
Mikado................................ 121

Minerva 50, 121
Minnesota 122
Minor Block 118
Mirror Plate 78
Mitered Prisms 175
Mochness 122
Model No. 857 138
Model No. 907 168
Modiste 124
Moon and Star 122
Moon and Star Variant 103
Moon and Star Variation 103
Moon and Star with Waffle 157
Moon and Star with Waffle Stem 103
Moss Rose 128
Nail 123
Nailhead 79
Nailhead Variant 161
National No. 600 136
Near Cut 126
Near Cut Daisy 34
Near Cut No. 2692 34
Near Cut No. 2699 35
Near Cut No. 2760 34
Nemesis 170
Neptune 143
Nevada 123
New Era 124
New Grand 81
New Hampshire 124
New Jersey 124
New Martinsville No. 110 186
New Martinsville No. 711 109
New Martinsville No. 718 76
New Mexico 14
Nickel-Plate No. 27 74
Nickel-Plate No. 76 149
No. 12 Line 126
No. 44 33
No. "45" 165
No. 75 – Square 125
No. 76 Ware 76
No. 89 147
No. 100 38
No. 119 125
No. 126 134
No. 153 151
No. 228 13
No. 276 43
No. 292 186
No. 292 Pattern 107
No. 500 164
No. 575 Fostoria Glass 37
No. 600 146
No. 702 111
No. 716 – "Rebecca" 101
No. 717 93
No. 720 47
No. 800 Fine Cut Four Panel 88
No. 1229 75
No. 1235 22
No. 1280 184
No. 1295 19
No. 1300 87
No. 1333 168
No. 2500 186
No. 2500 Cambridge 40
No. 15067 171
No. 15083 37
Nogi 125
Northwood Hobstar 126
Notched Finecut 132
Oak Leaf 183
Oats and Barley 182
O'Hara Diamond 126
O'Hara No. 82 – Crown Jewels .. 39
O'Hara's Diamond 126
Ohio 127
Ohio Flint No. 92 129
Ohio Flint No. 808 6
Ohio Star 127
Old Abe 77
Old Man 143
Old Man of the Mountain(s) 179
Old Man of the Woods 143
Olympia 154
Oneata 128
One Hundred and One 128
One-o-One 128
Open Rose 128
Opera 6
Optic 12
Oregon 129
Orient 30, 157
Orinda 129
Orion 37
Ornate Star 130
Oval Loop 144
Overall Diamond 168
Paddlewheel 130
Paden City No. 205 44
Paden City No. 206 100
Paisley 24
Paisley with Dots 24
Palace 122
Panama 130
Paneled Cherry 40
Paneled Daisy 131, 132
Paneled Diamond Cut and Fan 85
Paneled English Hobnail with Prisms 116
Paneled Flower 114
Paneled 44 146
Paneled Herringbone 72
Paneled Palm 131
Paneled Sprig 162
Paneled Stippled Flower 114
Paneled Thistle 132
Paneled Thousand Eye 172
Panelled Daisy and Button 132
Panelled Daisy and Fine Cut 97
Panelled Diamond Cross 88
Panelled Diamonds and Finecut 37
Panelled English Hobnail 132
Panelled Grape 133
Panelled Heather 134
Panelled Iris 171
Panelled Jewel 121
Panelled Strawberry 135
Panelled Thumbprint 136
Panelled Zipper 100
Panel Rib and Shell 131
Parachute 136
Paragon 35
Paris 186
Parthenon 62
Patricia 59
Pattee Cross 136
Pattern 705 157
Pattern 730 131
Pattern 876 61
Peacock Eye 80
Peacock Feather(s) 80
Pearl 137
Pearl, Huntington's 137
Pendant 125
Pennsylvania 137
Perfection 174
Persian 27, 49
Pigmy 174
Pillar and Cut Diamond 175
Pillow and Sunburst 138
Pillow Encircled 138
Pinafore 6
Pineapple 100
Pineapple & Fan 138
Pinwheel 36
Pioneer 182
Pioneer No. 9 26
Pioneer's No. 21 139
Pioneer's No. 250 145
Plain Band 139
Pleat and Panel 140
Pleat and Tuck 7
Plume 140
Pointed Bull's Eye 147
Pointed Jewel 141
Pointed Jewels 141
Popcorn 141
Portland 142
Portland with Diamond Point 179
Posies and Pods 142
Post Script 143
Potted Plant 73
Prayer Mat 81
Prayer Rug 81
Primrose 143
Prince's Feather 68
Priscilla 53, 181
Prism and Herringbone 72
Prison Window(s) 94
Proud Lion 110
Queen Anne 143
Queen's Necklace 111
Question Mark 144
Quintec 144
Rabbit Tracks 136
Radiant Daisy 158
Rainbow Variant 33
Ranson 144
Ranson 500 144
Rebecca at the Well 15
Recessed Pillar – Red Top 123
Recessed Pillar – Thumbprint Band 123
Red Block 145
Red Block and Lattice 26
Red Loop & Fine Cut 124
Red Loop & Finecut 124
Red Sunflower 34
Regina 145
Reticulated Cord 146
Reverse 44 146
Reverse Torpedo 147
Ribbed Droplet Band 147
Ribbed Ellipse 148
Ribbon 77
Ribbon Candy 148
Richards & Hartley No. 25 172
Richards & Hartley No. 55 144
Richards & Hartley No. 500 50
Richards & Hartley No. 525 – Proud Lion 110
Richards & Hartley's Oregon .. 158
Richmond (Nickel-Plate) 149
Rising Sun 149
Riverside 65
Riverside No. 492 64
Roanoke 150
Robin Hood 150
Robinson No. 1 67
Robinson No. 129 34
Rock Crystal 150
Roman Medallion 121
Roman Rosette 151
Romola 151
Rose Point Band 151
Rosette Medallion 69
Roughneck 186
Royal Crystal 169
Ruby Rosette 89
Ruby Thumbprint 105
Ruby Thumbprint – Clear 105
Santa Claus 143
Sawtooth 10
Sawtooth and Star 126
Sawtooth Band 10
Sawtoothed Honeycomb 152
Sawtooth Honeycomb 152
Scalloped Band 152
Scalloped Daisy – Red Top 32
Scalloped Diamond 32
Scalloped Diamond – Red Top. 32
Scalloped Lines 152
Scalloped Six Point 152
Scalloped Skirt 153
Scrolls with Bull's Eye 170
Scroll with Cane Band 153
Scroll with Flowers 154
Seagrit 39
"Seashell" 17
Seedpod 154
Seely 74
Serrated Block & Loop 152
Serrated Rib and Fine Cut 155
Sextec 155
Sharp Oval and Diamond 113
Sheaf and Diamond 155
"Shell and Scroll" 80
Shell and Spike 156
Shell and Tassel 156
Shell and Tassel – Square 156
Sheraton 156
Shield 32
Shield Band 11
Shining Diamonds 169
Shoshone 156
Shrine 157
Siamese Necklace 116
Silver Queen 157
Simple Frosted Ribbon 15
Simplicity 157

Single Scallop.................... 132
Six Point Star......................... 23
Skilton................................. 158
Slewed Horseshoe 158
Small Block and Prism 27
Small Comet......................... 159
Snail.................................... 159
Snowflower.......................... 159
Solar 160
Spades 120
Spartan 164
Spatula 160
Spear Point......................... 141
Spearpoint Band 119
Spirea 161
Spirea Band......................... 161
Sprig 162
Square and Dot 161
Squared Dot 161
Square Lion 75
Square Lion Heads................. 75
Squat Pineapple 163
Star 61, 126
Star and Crescent 163
Star and Dewdrop 56
Star and Diamonds............... 119
Star and Punty..................... 122
Star Band 163
Star Burst 23
Star Galaxy 61
Star in Bull's Eye.................. 164
Star in Diamond.................... 164
Star of David........................ 164
Star of the East 93
Starred Block....................... 165
Starred Jewel 113
Starred Loop 165
Starry Night 125
Steimer's Diamond 152
Stelle.................................... 53
Stemless Daisy 48
Stippled Dahlia 51
Stippled Daisy 165, 183
Stippled Dart & Balls 166
Stippled Double Loop 166
Stippled Forget-Me-Not 166
Stippled Oval 62
Stippled Paneled Flower 114
Stippled Primrose........... 114, 143
Stippled Sandbar 167
Stippled Star Variant.............. 167
Strawberry and Bird 24
Strawberry with Roman Key... 135
Sun and Star 53
Sunbeam 167
Sunk Jewel 113
Sunrise 149
Swirl.................................... 68
Swirled Column 22
Swirl(s) and Feather(s) 68
Swiss................................... 7
Sydney................................ 168
Sylvan................................. 168
Tacoma 168
Tarentum Harvard 86
Tarentum No. 240 160
Tarentum No. 300 114

Tarentum's Atlanta 169
Tarentum's Hartford................ 87
Tarentum Star 130
Tarentum's Virginia................ 169
Teardrop and Diamond Block... 12
Teepee 170
Tennessee............................ 170
Teutonic 171
Texas 171
Theatrical............................... 6
Thistle and Sunflower............ 183
Thistleblow 171
Thompson No. 18.................. 29
Thompson No. 77.................. 175
Thompson's No. 17 174
Thousand Eye Three Panel..... 172
Thread Band 172
Three-In-One 173
Three Knob........................... 6
Three Panel 172
Three Stories 27
Thumbnail 173
Thumbprint and Prisms........... 11
Thumbprint Band – Clear 52
Thumbprint Band – Red Top 52
Thumbprint Panel 136
Tidal................................... 174
Tiny Lion 110
Tippecanoe.......................... 182
Tobin.................................. 109
Toltec 174
Tooth and Claw 65
Torpedo 174
Triple Triangle 175
Triple Triangle – Red Top 175
Triple X 168
Trump 175
Truncated Cube.................... 175
Tulip Petals 40
Tulip with Sawtooth 176
Twin Pear 15
Twin Teardrop 176
Union's Radiant 152
U.S. Diamond Block............... 59
U.S. Glass No. 85 – New Floral.. 25
U.S. Glass No. 414 164
U.S. Glass No. 900 85
U.S. Glass No. 1010.............. 148
U.S. Glass No. 9525.............. 107
U.S. Glass No. 15001 126
U.S. Glass No. 15002 123
U.S. Glass No. 15006 141
U.S. Glass No. 15007 – Horn of
    Plenty............................. 77
U.S. Glass No. 15009 72
U.S. Glass No. 15014 88
U.S. Glass No. 15025 59
U.S. Glass No. 15028 112
U.S. Glass No. 15029 94
U.S. Glass No. 15030 151
U.S. Glass No. 15038 63
U.S. Glass No. 15043 69
U.S. Glass No. 15046 – Victor... 156
U.S. Glass No. 15048 137
U.S. Glass No. 15048½
    – Pennsylvania.................. 137

U.S. Glass No. 15049 118
U.S. Glass No. 15050 127
U.S. Glass No. 15051 –
    Kentucky 104
U.S. Glass No. 15052 93
U.S. Glass No. 15053 –
    Louisiana 113
U.S. Glass No. 15054 –
    Massachusetts 119
U.S. Glass No. 15055 –
    Minnesota 122
U.S. Glass No. 15056 – Florida... 72
U.S. Glass No. 15057 –
    Colorado........................... 45
U.S. Glass No 15059 33
U.S. Glass No. 15060 –
    Vermont 178
U.S. Glass No. 15062 – Alabama ..8
U.S. Glass No 15064 –
    Tennessee........................ 170
U.S. Glass No. 15065 –
    Delaware........................... 55
U.S. Glass No 15066 114
U.S. Glass No. 15067 – Texas . 171
U.S. Glass No. 15068 46
U.S. Glass No. 15069 100
U.S. Glass No. 15070 – New
    Jersey............................. 124
U.S. Glass No. 15071 –
    Virginia............................ 179
U.S. Glass No. 15072 –
    Kansas............................ 104
U.S. Glass No. 15073 –
    Oregon............................ 129
U.S. Glass No. 15074 180
U.S. Glass No. 15075 123
U.S. Glass No. 15076 – Georgia. 80
U.S. Glass No. 15077 –
    Michigan........................... 121
U.S. Glass No. 15078 –
    New York 115
U.S. Glass No. 15081 –
    Wyoming 184
U.S. Glass No. 15084 – New
    Hampshire 124
U.S. Glass No. 15085............. 22
U.S. Glass No. 15086 – Mirror... 78
U.S. Glass No. 15088 130
U.S. Glass No. 15090 31
U.S. Glass No. 15091 12
U.S. Glass No. 15092 164
U.S. Glass No. 15094 36
U.S. Glass No. 15098 176
U.S. Glass No. 15101 33
U.S. Glass No. 15105 117
U.S. Glass No. 15108 163
U.S. Glass No. 15110
    – Sunshine....................... 149
U.S. Glass No. 15111 158
U.S. Glass No. 15112 136
U.S. Glass No. 15116 160
U.S. Glass No. 15117 –
    Newport............................ 31
U.S. Glass No. 15118 35
U.S. Glass No. 15121 142
U.S. Glass No. 15123 74
U.S. Glass No. 15125 98

U.S. Glass No. 15131 66
U.S. Glass No. 15134 63
U.S. Glass No. 15135............. 159
U.S. Glass No. 15140 –
    Athenia 146
U.S. Glass No. 15145 44
U.S. Glass No. 15147 73
U.S. Glass No. 15150 46
U.S. Glass No. 15155 106
U.S. Mirror 78
U.S. Peacock....................... 158
U.S. Portland 142
U.S. Regal 176
U.S. Sheraton 177
Valencia Waffle 177
Venus 111
Vera 67
Vermont 178
Vermont Honeycomb............. 178
Verona 179
Versailles.............................. 178
Victoria................................ 178
Viking 130, 179
V In Heart............................. 177
Virginia 78, 179
Virginia – 140 145
Vogue 153
Waffle and Fine Cut 37
Waffle and Star Band 179
Waffle – Red Top 91
Washboard 7
Washington (U.S. Glass) 180
Waterlily 151
Waverly 180
Wedding Bells....................... 180
West Virginia's No. 213.......... 153
Westmoreland 181
Westmoreland Block 181
Westmoreland No. 550 91
Westmoreland's Priscilla......... 181
Westward Ho 182
Wetzel 164
Wheat and Barley 182
Whirligig.............................. 33
Whitton 88
Wigwam.............................. 170
Willow and Oak 183
Willow Oak 183
Wiltec 183
Winged Scroll 184
Winged Scrolls 112
Winking Eye 67
Wishbone 99
Woodrow 78
Wreath 82
Wyoming 184
XLCR 105
X-Ray 185
Yale 185
Yoke and Circle 124
Yutec 185
Zipper Cross 186
Zippered Heart 186
Zipper Slash 186